Fellowship of
Reason

FELLOWSHIP OF REASON

A Moral Community for the 21st Century

Martin L. Cowen III

COPYRIGHT © 2001 BY MARTIN L. COWEN III.

LIBRARY OF CONGRESS NUMBER: 2001116392
ISBN #:   HARDCOVER   0-7388-6232-0
         SOFTCOVER   0-7388-6233-9

All rights reserved. No part of this book shall be reproduced, stored in a retrieval system, or transmitted by any means, electronic, mechanical, photocopying, recording, or otherwise, without written permission from the author.

No copyright claim is made to the work of others. The work of others is quoted in this book with appropriate acknowledgment of the sources in reliance upon the "fair use" doctrine.

Scripture taken from the Holy Bible, New International Version. Copyright © 1973, 1978, 1984 by International Bible Society. Used by permission of Zondervan Publishing House. All rights reserved.

The "NIV" and "New International Version" trademarks are registered in the United States Patent and Trademark Office by the International Bible Society. Use of either trademark requires the permission of the International Bible Society.

Fellowship of Reason is a service mark registered in the United States Patent and Trademark Office and owned by Martin Lindsey Cowen III.

For more information about the Fellowship of Reason visit our website at www.kindreason.com.

This book was printed in the United States of America.

CONTENTS

Introduction 14
Chapter 1—Reasons for Being 18
   Fellowship 19
   Celebration 20
   Personal Reflection 21
   Reorientation with Moral Values 24
   Enjoyment of Art 26
   Ethics 28
      Teaching morality 28
      Preserving moral knowledge 29
      Integrated world view 30
   Conclusion 32

Chapter 2—The Value of Human Life 33
   Different Views 34
   Individual Human Life Is the Ultimate Value 35
   Human Life Is More than
      Survival at Any Price 36
   There Are No Conflicts of Interest
      Among Rational Men 39
   Historical Consequences of Other Views 41
   Ours Is a Philosophy for Living on Earth 41

Chapter 3—What is the Meaning of Your Life? 43
   Not "What Is the Meaning of Life?" But "What Is the
      Meaning of My Life?" 45
   Life and Happiness 45
   Three Senses of Meaning 46
   What Is the Meaning of Your Life Today? 47
   Life "Time" Inventory 49

Sleep 49
Personal maintenance 49
Career 49
Television 50
Health and fitness 50
Art, music, and reading 51
Self-improvement and hobbies 51
Friends 52
Marriage 52
Children 52
Spiritual exercise 53
Planning 53
Summary of time inventory 54
Evaluation of Life "Time" Inventory 54
Your days are numbered 54
Imbalances 56
Don't waste time 56
These are personal choices 57

Chapter 4—Your Personal Destiny 59
You Won the Lottery! 60
The Problem of Survival
 and the Problem of Meaning 61
More Clues to Your Personal
 Mission in Life 62
Who are your heroes? 62
What are your hobbies? 63
What was your favorite subject in school? 63
What do you enjoy reading? 64
What are your pipe dreams? 64
What do you get excited about? 64
What are your particular talents? 64
Logotherapy 65
Professional help 65
Fulfilling Your Personal Destiny
 Is the Meaning of Your Life 65
The Definitive Statement of the
 Purpose of My Life 66
Pitfalls to avoid 67

Parents 68
Your peer group and "low" jobs 68
The media and the "proper" lifestyle 69
A job as a means to your ends 71
Changing Personal Missions 72
Use Gradualism 72
A World Full of People
  Following Their Bliss 73
Wholeness, Harmony, Radiance 73

Chapter 5—The Human Soul 75
Hubris 76
Anger 77
Fear 78
Discovering One's Soul 79
  The other 79
  Your daemon 79
  Reason 81
  Emotions 82
  Your parents' child 83
  Conclusion to discovering one's soul 83
The Stages of Life 83
  Childhood 84
  Adolescence 85
  Adulthood 86
  Old age/Decrepitude 88
  Conclusion to stages of life 88
Immortality 89

Chapter 6—Spiritual Exercise 90
Examination of Conscience (Past) 93
Experience of Repressed Pain (Past) 95
Look the Devil in the Face (Future) 97
Death (Future) 98
Daily Spiritual Exercise 99
  The notebook 100
Conclusion 101

Chapter 7—Our Philosophy of Reason 103
Axioms 104
Corollaries of Axioms 105
Man's Nature 106
Morality 106
Man and Society 108
Art 108

Chapter 8—The Virtues of Benevolence 110
What Is the Difference? 110
Loving Family, Good Friends,
   Vital Community 110
   Generosity *111*
   Tolerance and independence *115*
   Moral judgment and tolerance *118*
   Sensitivity *121*
The Penalty for Lacking Virtue 122
Human Brotherhood and the Family of Man 123
Emergency Aid 124
   The sense that life is worth living *126*
   The sense that one is worth living *127*
   The sense that one is capable of living *128*
   Summary on emergency aid *128*
Empathy as a Root of the
   Virtues of Benevolence 129
Altruism's Mistakes 130
Benevolence and Trading Partners 133
Conclusion 133

Chapter 9—Celebration 134
Introduction 134
Discipline and Ritual 135
Selective Focus of Attention 135
   Celebration of freedom *136*
   Celebration of visitors *137*
   Celebration of each other *137*
   Celebratory announcements *137*
   Celebration of art *137*

Celebration of heroes 138
Celebration of amateur talent 138
Oratory 138
Celebration of personal mission 138
Reflection, mindful meditations, or spiritual exercise . 139
Glass is half-full as philosophic principle 139
Emotional Goals of Celebration 139

Chapter 10—Rational Rituals 143
Life Is Precious 143
Stages of Life 144
  Celebrations of pregnancy and birth 144
  Transition from infancy to childhood 145
  Puberty:The teenage ritual 147
    Lessons 1 and 2: What Is Love? 148
    Lessons 3 and 4: Self-Sufficiency 148
    Lessons 5 and 6: Career Planning 149
    Lessons 7 and 8: Sex, Birth Control, and STDs ... 149
    Lessons 9 and 10: What Is Marriage? 149
    Lesson 11: Parenting 150
    Lesson 12: Conclusion 150
  Marriage 150
  Parenting 151
  Midlife changes 151
  Death 152
Lesser Rituals 152
  Bless you 152
  Reflections prior to dining 152
  Reflections upon retiring for the evening 153
  Anniversaries, birthdays, and graduations 154
  Winter solstice/Christmas 154
  Vernal equinox/Easter 154
  Independence Day 155
  Thanksgiving 155
  Oaths 155
Conclusion 155

Chapter 11 — Mythology ... 156
Heroes ... 156
The Functions of Mythology ... 157
- *Mystical* ... *158*
- *Cosmological* ... *158*
- *Sociological* ... *158*
- *Pedagogical* ... *158*

The Hero's Journey ... 159
- *Ordinary world* ... *159*
- *Call to adventure* ... *160*
- *Refusing the call* ... *161*
  - *Adolescence* ... *161*
  - *Half-way Decisions* ... *162*
  - *Full Acceptance — Gattaca* ... *163*
  - *The Completion of an Adventure* ... *164*
  - *Loss of Relationship* ... *164*
  - *Accidental Loss* ... *165*
  - *Full Acceptance of Santiago* ... *165*
- *Crossing the first threshold* ... *167*
  - *Fear of Rejection or Failure* ... *167*
  - *Your Parents* ... *168*
  - *Self-Imposed Expectations* ... *168*
  - *Crippling Pain* ... *169*
- *Finding a mentor* ... *169*
- *Enduring the supreme ordeal* ... *170*
- *Returning with the elixir* ... *171*

Conclusion ... 172

Chapter 12 — What's In It for Me? ... 173
Sacred Being ... 174
Now Moments ... 174
Written Life Plan ... 175
Friends ... 176
Entertainment ... 176
Long Range Values ... 176
Spread Freedom and Happiness ... 177
Home ... 177
- *The nature of home* ... *178*
- *A cultural institution* ... *179*

Appendix—Non-theism 181
  Negative Reasons for Theism 182
    Faith of our fathers 182
    It is the thing to do 182
    Infantilism 183
    Fear of death 183
  Positive Reasons for Theism 184
    Christianity and individualism 185
    Mystery and wonder of the universe 188
    Personal experience of god 191
    Fear of irremediable injustice 192
    Love or grace 193
    Unitive experience 193
    Church for the children 193
  The Greatest Obstacle to Non-theism:
    God-Esteem 194
  Dissembling Non-theists 195
  Non-theists v. Atheists 195
  Faith v. Reason 196

References 197

THIS BOOK IS DEDICATED TO MY WIFE, LINDA, WITHOUT WHOSE LOVE, PATIENCE, INTEREST, AND SUPPORT THIS BOOK WOULD NOT HAVE BEEN POSSIBLE.

Introduction

The Fellowship of Reason is a rational moral community founded upon a philosophy of reason and upon the virtues of benevolence.

Members of the Fellowship of Reason have two things in common. First, our goal is life on earth, or more specifically, health and happiness. Health and happiness are the physical and psychological manifestations of life. Second, our means of achieving life—health and happiness—is reason. We gather together regularly to celebrate the events of our lives, enjoy literature, art, and music, share fellowship, study ethics, reorient with our self-selected hierarchy of values, and privately reflect upon our lives. Until the creation of the Fellowship of Reason, only religious institutions performed all of these functions. In our rational moral community there is no reference to a god, unthinking faith, unquestioning obedience to authority, or other unearthly matters. The Fellowship of Reason is concerned only with the universe perceivable by our senses and by the tools science invents to augment our senses.

Our philosophy of reason is based upon the premise that the universe exists independently of any consciousness and that we exist, possess consciousness, and can perceive and know that universe, including moral laws, by our faculty of reason. Ethics is neither an edict nor arbitrary. Ethics is a science.

The virtues of benevolence, never appreciated for their value to the individual's survival by any institution before the Fellowship of Reason, are necessary to achieve through trade and other voluntary relations the values owned by and embodied in other individuals. Individual human beings are, in our view, the source of all values. An awareness of the means to achieve successful human relations is crucial to life.

For almost two millennia religions have had a virtual monopoly on morality. No longer. Today, there is a philosophy of reason that provides a rational and objective validation of moral laws. The Fellowship of Reason exists to advocate, celebrate, and promulgate that morality based upon reality to a literate, thoughtful, reality-oriented, self-responsible general public worldwide.

This book is divided into twelve chapters. Chapter 1 elaborates the reasons for the existence of our rational moral community. The objective human needs that until now have been served only by religion are explored. In chapter 2 I explain the details of our moral philosophy by identifying what we regard as the ultimate value. The choices of ultimate value include God, the state, the environment, and individual human life. Chapter 3 considers the meaning of life from three angles—the purpose or goal of life, the intention of life, and the actual definition of a particular human life as manifested in the actions taken by that individual. We work through an exercise to discover the meaning (definition) of the reader's life. Chapter 4 advocates that each individual discover and deliberately pursue his or her own major lifetime goals, that he or she give his or her life a meaning in the sense of purpose or goal. Happiness, we hold, requires a life purpose. Chapter 5 considers the contents of human consciousness. Five components of the human soul are explored—the other, your daemon, reason, emotions, and your parents' child. Chapter 6 presents techniques for working on your soul and explains the nonmystical, natural referents of the Holy Trinity. Chapter 7 concisely states our philosophy of reason. Chapter 8 introduces the new component to our philosophy of reason—benevolence. The relationship between the virtues of benevolence and the penultimate values of a loving family, good friends, and community is revealed. Chapter 9 details the elements of a regular meeting of the Fellowship of Reason. Chapter 10 describes our rational rituals. In order to be happy, one must selectively focus one's attention. These rituals are institutionally structured disciplines designed to focus our attention upon the good things in life. Chapter 11 reveals the mythology of our new moral community. And finally, in chapter 12 we provide reasons why you should create a Fellowship of Reason in your city. We show how reason, if utilized consistently as the means of living, will spread human freedom, prosperity, and happiness throughout the world. An appendix concludes, addressed to our theistic friends.

The purpose of morality is to teach you to enjoy yourself and live well on earth. Reason makes human life possible. The Fellowship of Reason proposes to bring to you, in regular weekly celebrations and in daily spiritual exercises, tools that will enhance your life and the lives of everyone around you. Read on to learn more about the Fellowship of Reason.

Chapter 1 — Reasons for Being

> Better to light one small candle than to curse the darkness.
> —Chinese Proverb
>
> Come now, let us reason together. ——Isaiah 1:18
>
> What has been will be again, what has been done will be done again; there is nothing new under the sun.
> —Ecclesiastes 1:9

I write this book to satisfy a need I have felt since my teenage years, when I resigned my membership in the Presbyterian Church with the words, "I am an atheist." As you will see, I have not changed my mind and become a theist. In fact with the passage of time I have become, if anything, more certain of my non-theism. (Today, I call myself a non-theist, rather than an atheist.) I have, though, come to realize that the community of friends and benevolent people I enjoyed in church provided many values that are missing from my life today.

I believe there are millions of people in the world like me—people who go to church for those (as yet undefined) values, while harboring secret doubts about Christian dogma, and others who forego the values, because they cannot feign a faith they do not share in order to belong.

Now after thirty years outside the church, I undertake to discover what true values religion provides and whether those values might somehow be separated from the foolishness. By foolishness I mean magic (my word) or miracles (the religious word), Original Sin, the devaluation of human life and consciousness, and the religious ethic of self-sacrifice.

There are nearly 5 billion people in the world today claiming some religious affiliation. It is obvious that religion serves some genuine human needs. Just what those needs are is the topic of this chapter. Once we have identified them, we will know the reasons for the existence of the Fellowship of Reason.

FELLOWSHIP

A fellowship, as an organization, is a community of persons having similar values, interests, and tastes. Fellowship, as a personal experience, is the enjoyment of the company of people of like mind and values. The need for fellowship is one of the most important objective human needs served by religion.

Psychologist Nathaniel Branden, Ph.D., explains why we are motivated to seek out other human beings whom we can value and love: "Man desires and needs the experience of self-awareness that results from perceiving his self as an objective existent—and he is able to achieve this experience through interaction with the consciousness of other living entities (Branden 1971, p. 202)."

It is in fellowship with friends of like mind and values that we can best see of ourselves. This is often referred to as the principle of psychological visibility. We are able to experience *ourselves* as valuable and objective entities in the world through our interaction with others. In addition, we are able to experience *our* values manifested in the persons of these others.

Aristotle (384–322 BCE) recognized the importance of fellowship: "[I]t is consciousness of oneself as good that makes existence desirable, and such consciousness is pleasant in itself. Therefore a man ought also to share his friend's consciousness of his existence, and this is attained by their living together and by conversing and communicating their thoughts to each other... Therefore to be happy a man needs virtuous friends (Aristotle, *Ethics*, p. 565)."

Religions serve the genuine human need for fellowship in tens of thousands of churches, synagogues, mosques, and temples in America. There is a creed for everyone and within each creed there are numerous local options allowing those of the same social and economic classes to worship together.

MARTIN L. COWEN III

In regions serious about religion, for example in the Bible Belt of the American South, a church member can spend over seven hours in religious activities every week. A full-service Southern Baptist church has an early service on Sunday morning, followed by Sunday school, followed by a late morning service. On Sunday evening, classes on various subjects such as finance, prayer, church missions, divorce recovery, and single parenthood may be offered. On Wednesday nights, supper is offered, followed by choir practice. At other times during the week, intramural sports, such as basketball, are played in the church gymnasium. The opportunities for fellowship with persons of like mind and values in this environment are enormous.

The Fellowship of Reason also will provide such fellowship. One day soon, we will bring together in weekly meetings reality-oriented individuals numbering in the hundreds. We will offer regular classes by rational experts in their fields on subjects like career planning, marriage and family, parenting, finance, and retirement. Weekly intramural sports, Wednesday night suppers, Sunday school, and daycare are all anticipated. Think how much richer our lives will be with so many opportunities to experience psychological visibility.

CELEBRATION

Religions have many rituals, the purpose of which is to celebrate life. Members of the Fellowship of Reason, being rational individualists, can appreciate the importance of celebrating our lives and our families.

The creation of a child is a sacred human endeavor. (Sacred means pertaining to the highest of human values.) The religious ritual of baptism is an opportunity for proud parents to dress themselves and their newborn child in their Sunday best. The trio—father, mother, and child—appear before their extended family and friends in the church sanctuary. They are singled out, brought forward, and their greatest happiness, the birth of their child, is publicly celebrated. Afterward, pictures are taken and everyone admires and praises the infant.

Bat mitzvahs, bar mitzvahs, and confirmations mark the passage from childhood to adolescence. This crossing from the innocence of childhood to awareness of adult sexuality is one of the most difficult and ecstatic of human transitions. It is objectively valuable to the adolescent undergoing the transformation to be informed about what she or he can expect. It is appropriate to celebrate this most profound of experiences. The adult celebrants are reminded of their own time of sexual awakening. The attention and the celebration inform the adolescent celebrants that *something great* is about to happen.

Graduation ceremonies mark significant achievements after years of hard study. Religions routinely celebrate these important events.

Marriage is one of the three most important commitments a person can make. (Children and career are the other two.) It is crucial that this lifetime commitment be solemnized in a formal ceremony.

Finally, upon the death of a loved one, it is appropriate to have a ceremony honoring and celebrating the life of the decedent and acknowledging the decedent's value to the bereaved.

The objective purpose of all of these ceremonies is to communicate to the partic ipants: "Pay attention to your life. *This* event of your life is important. Think about it. Know what you are doing. Your life is precious. Honor, respect, and enjoy it."

Religion performs all of these ceremonies. The Fellowship of Reason proposes analogous, but rational, rituals to mark the times of our lives. Chapters 9 and 10 describe and explain our special celebrations and rituals.

Personal Reflection

Since reason informs us that there is no god to whom you can pray, members of the Fellowship of Reason may ask if the religious activity of prayer has any rational value. Yet, millions pray. Prayer is a directed process of thought. Rational individualists will recognize that directed thought is the essence of reason. Let us examine prayer for objective value.

One of the main activities of a religious person is prayer, a regular meditation. A prayer can confess a sin or request forgiveness for having sinned. The superficial and mystical purpose of this prayer is to receive divine absolution. This purpose is fantasy and wishful thinking. There is, however, an objectively valuable use for this type of prayer.

The objectively valuable use of a prayer for forgiveness is to concentrate the sinner's attention upon what he has done. One hopes that the sinner will use that attention to determine what to do to *correct* the sin and to make *amends* for it. The only way to achieve "forgiveness" is (1) to correct the fault (restitution), if possible, (2) to suffer an appropriate consequence (retribution), (3) to resolve (repentance) personally never to commit the fault again and to make that resolve evident, and (4) to take action (such as amending one's faulty moral code) to ensure non-repetition (reformation). As an example, suppose you have shoplifted a CD from a retail outlet. You should (1) correct the fault by returning the disc or offering to pay for it; (2) offer yourself for criminal prosecution and punishment; (3) apologize to your victim; and, (4) seek counseling to determine and to correct what is wrong with your hierarchy of values. Now *that* is seeking forgiveness. Forgiveness involves four "R's": restitution, retribution, repentance, and reformation.

A prayer can request a benefit from a personal god. "Dear God, please keep my spouse and our children safe. Amen." Or "Dear God, I have lost my job and I must find another soon. I must support my family. What am I going to do? Please help me. Amen."

A religious person may actually expect the protection prayer to bring results. However, a thoughtful religious person will recognize, often with perplexity, that members of his sect, with the same regularity as non-religious persons, suffer the tragedies of life. The expectation of beneficial results simply from the pronouncement of the protection prayer is superstition.

However, the protection prayer accompanied by action can have objective value. Consider how the protection prayer might bring some actual advantage to the supplicant and the intended beneficiary of the prayer: If the protection prayer brings the reality-oriented issues of personal safety into the mind of the person praying, her mind, now focused on this important subject, can make important connections or realize some important facts. She might suddenly remember that the reason she is worried about her adult daughter's safety in that new apartment complex is that she noticed a suspicious-looking man lurking near her daughter's car in the parking lot last night. Because of this recollection, she might immediately call her daughter and encourage her to be especially cautious going to and from the car, making sure to go only when other people are present. This protection prayer with resulting action can bring a real benefit. Of course, the cause of the benefit is the focused mind of the person praying, not her personal god.

It is of objective value to consider the safety of loved ones. Good things can happen when you consider the matter, even if there is no personal god to extend protection to your loved ones.

The prayer for a specific benefit, such as a new job, can also have objective value. The directing of one's focused attention toward one's personal problems and concerns is of objective value. The prayer that asks for assistance can serve this objective value.

The objective value served is the calling of the human mind into action to resolve the problem or concern. There is, after all, no other way in reality to solve problems than for the mind of a human being to engage in the process of problem solving.

When a person regularly prays to her personal god for assistance in finding a new job, she focuses her mind on the subject of the search for a new job. When that magnificent fact of existence the human mind does its work and solves the problem, it is *not* the religious person's personal god who deserves thanks.

To the extent that prayer leads one's mind to solve problems through reason, even if that is not the intention of the person praying, prayer serves an objective human need. In fact, a person who prays may have an advantage over a person who does not pray, if the person who does not pray does not have a meaningful substitute for prayer. In other words, the person who regularly focuses his mind (by the use of prayer) upon the problems and concerns of his life is more likely to think about and solve those problems than a person who does not regularly focus his mind upon the challenges and opportunities confronting him.

Busy people rarely set aside time for personal reflection. People need a ritual to focus their attention upon the activities and problems of their lives. Religion serves this important human need. The Fellowship of Reason has developed several powerful spiritual exercises to serve this crucial need (chapter 6).

Reorientation with Moral Values

A weekly church service, such as the Catholic Mass, is the central feature of organized religion. Some of the characteristics of these services are recitals of creeds, public prayer, readings from the Bible, a sermon, and hymns. A major function of these services is to remind the religious person of her chosen set of rules for living and to return her mind to her chosen life path, to her life's purpose and meaning. The recitation of creeds and prayers, the reading of stories illustrative of the rules, the delivery of a didactic lecture, and the singing of the meaningful words of hymns, all organized to a specific theme, fulfill this function. The religious person is reminded of her chosen *principles* for living.

Everyone on some level understands the importance of acting on principle. For example, consider the case of a teenage boy who would like to date a particular teenage girl. The question for the boy is how to persuade the girl to go out with him. The answer, though the boy need not identify the issue in these terms, are principles, the principles of dating. The boy will discover that paying attention to the girl at school one day and ignoring her the next gets him nowhere. He identifies the principle that he should consistently pay attention to the girl. He will discover that if the type of attention he pays is courteous and kind one day and rude and vicious the next, his cause is not advanced. He identifies the principle that he should be consistently courteous and kind to the girl. He will discover that if he has poor personal hygiene and fails to dress within the styles acceptable in his culture, the girl resists even his consistent, courteous, and kind attentions. He learns the principle that cleanliness and stylish dress are important to the achievement of his goal. In short, he learns he must follow certain specific rules, that he must act on principle, if he is to achieve his goal.

The achievement of all human values requires that a person act on principle. Each of us must discover or be taught those principles.

The religions of the world have developed highly sophisticated sets of rules for living. Typically, people are taught these systems of principles from birth first by their parents and then by religious and educational institutions.

It is objectively valuable to be reminded of the principles by which you live. Just as the teenage boy who is trying to get a date will appreciate his mother's reminder to brush his teeth and comb his hair before going to school and encountering his intended girlfriend, so everyone can appreciate being reminded of the important principles by which we have chosen to live.

Religion provides a template for the "proper" life. Religion has an answer to the ultimate question: What is the meaning of life? Take, for example, the Catholic Church. In brief, the Catholic template for life is: worship God, marry, be faithful to your spouse, have as many little Catholics as you can, work hard, tithe, and prepare yourself for your eternal reward in heaven. A faithful Catholic does not have the problem that non-religious people have: What will be the meaning of my life and how will I achieve that meaning? Life for a faithful Catholic is not nearly so complex. The Church supplies the answers.

By regularly attending Mass or another religious service the faithful are constantly reminded of their life path, of their hierarchy of values. True, the hierarchy of values is the church's template. Nevertheless, they are reminded of their path, and the faithful can check to make sure they are on their path.

It is crucially important to be reminded of your life path, of your hierarchy of values, on a regular, daily basis. Living your life is a full-time job and there are no days off. Any step off your path is a meaningless and perhaps disastrous step. If careful attention is not paid, especially early in life, to choosing your purposes and adopting strategies and tactics for accomplishing them, missteps can set an irrevocable and unintended life path. For example, a child born out of wedlock to a teenaged girl can greatly limit that girl's life choices. She will be bound to the immediate problem of providing food, shelter, and clothing for her infant child. If she does not have the help of the child's father or of her own family, she will be committed to working long hours at low pay, at least in the beginning. The option of finishing high school or of going on to college will be temporarily and possibly forever foreclosed. Simple religious rules and taboos address these practical problems.

The Fellowship of Reason has developed technologies for assisting people with the task of defining their life purposes and thus providing their lives with meaning. Your hierarchy of values is the most important of structures, but for most people it only exists on an implicit level and is not consistently applied. Just as an entrepreneur writes out a business plan before commencing a new venture, so should everyone write out her own life plan, refer to it, and update it regularly. Religion provides this service for its adherents. It is a valuable service. The Fellowship of Reason will assist people who do not blindly accept the "faith of their fathers" and who wish to define the meaning and purpose of their own lives for themselves.

In short, the Fellowship of Reason will teach the importance of defining our life purposes and will give instruction on how to go about it. We will learn that we must check our own, self-defined hierarchy of values on a regular daily basis. The Fellowship of Reason has invented rational rituals to assist in these crucial tasks.

Enjoyment of Art

The religious experience *is* an aesthetic experience. An aesthetic experience is an experience pertaining to the enjoyment of art. Religion is a form of mythology, "an organization of images conceived as a rendition of the sense of life. . . [T]his sense is to be apprehended in two ways, namely: 1) the way of thought, and 2) the way of experience. As thought mythology approaches—or is a primitive prelude to—science; and as experience *it is precisely art* (Campbell 1976, p. 179)." [emphasis supplied]

As evidence that the religious experience is an aesthetic experience, observe that a traditional Catholic Mass contains many artistic elements. The event may occur in a cathedral. Cathedrals are among the greatest architectural achievements of mankind, with beautiful stained glass windows, ornate carvings and sculptures, elaborate paintings and portraits, and high vaulted ceilings. There may be a beautiful golden altar at the front of the sanctuary. Much of the great music of the world was composed with religious themes in mind. Music is an omnipresent element in religious ceremonies. Incense is waved among the congregation to involve the sense of smell. Beautiful literature and poetry is read to the congregation. Spectacular processions occur. The priest, the choir, and the attendants all wear beautiful and ornate costumes. During Communion, the Host is distributed to all who wish to taste it.

The Catholic Mass involves all the senses: sight, hearing, touch, taste, and smell. All of the arts, architecture, dance, drama, literature, music, painting, poetry, sculpture, storytelling, speech, winemaking, and fashion design, have been utilized to create an aesthetic experience *par excellence*. The Church and the artists who have served it have been perfecting this event for nearly two thousand years. Little wonder that faithful participants claim to experience God during Mass.

How can we explain our enjoyment of art? Ayn Rand wrote: "Art is a concretization of metaphysics. Art brings man's concepts to the perceptual level of his consciousness and allows him to grasp them directly, as if they were percepts. This is the psycho-epistemological function of art and the reason of its importance in man's life (and the crux of the Objectivist esthetics) (Rand 1975, p.20)." In a different essay she explains:

> Since a rational man's ambition is unlimited, since his pursuit and achievement of values is a lifelong process—and the higher the values, the harder the struggle—he needs a moment, an hour or some period of time in which he can experience the sense of his completed task, the sense of living in a universe where his values have been successfully achieved. It is like a moment of rest, a moment to gain fuel to move

farther. Art gives him that fuel; the pleasure of contemplating the objectified reality of one's own sense of life is the pleasure of feeling what it would be like to live in one's ideal world (Rand 1975, p. 38).

For rational individualists, the ideal world is one inhabited by benevolent, productive, self-responsible, rights-respecting individuals. Just such people inhabit the community of the Fellowship of Reason.

The art of the Fellowship of Reason is not as developed as is religious art. Religion has a two-thousand-year head start. Therefore, the creation of *artistic* weekly celebrations is one of our greatest opportunities.

ETHICS

Teaching morality

Religion's most important contribution to mankind is moral instruction. Religions provide moral codes and insist that you practice them. Religion teaches its followers how to live.

Children and novices need moral instruction. Adults and adepts need to be reminded of their moral values. I have already discussed the religious function of reorientation with moral values earlier in this chapter. The need of children for moral instruction is one of the most important reasons people go to church.

Morality and moral instruction are necessary because human beings do not live by instinct. Our consciousness is not hardwired to know automatically and infallibly what is good for us and what is bad. Yet in order to survive we must know it. This is the reason we need the science of ethics.

Religion has for millennia commanded a virtual monopoly on morality. The Fellowship of Reason now challenges that monopoly.

FELLOWSHIP OF REASON

Preserving moral knowledge

Religion as an institution has preserved hard-won moral knowledge. The information need not be rediscovered with each new generation. The holy books and writings of the world's major religions, Christianity (Bible), Islam (Koran), Hinduism (Veda), Buddhism (Book of the Dead), and Judaism (Torah) contain many important and useful moral lessons.

The Fellowship of Reason, as an institution, aspires to become a storehouse for a rational morality to be transmitted from generation to generation.

The full integration of our philosophy of reason is a recent achievement. Many of its tenets are ancient knowledge, for example, the contributions of Aristotle (384–322 BCE). The collection of these threads of wisdom from the past is one of the missions of the Fellowship of Reason.

As an illustration of the fact that supposedly "new" ideas are often quite old, consider our emphasis upon the importance of the mind and reason in light of these ancient texts suppressed as heresy by the early Christian church. The quotations are taken from "The Teachings of Silvanus" (Robinson 1990, p. 381).

> Your mind [is] a guiding principle. 85

> Bring in your guide and your teacher. The mind is the guide, but reason is the teacher. They will bring you out of destruction and dangers. 85

> Let holy reason become a torch in your mind. . . 86

> Make yourself noble-minded through good conduct. Obtain the austerity of good discipline. Judge yourself like a wise judge. 87

29

> The wretched man who goes through all these things will die because he does not have the mind, the helmsman. But he is like a ship which the wind tosses to and fro, and like a loose horse which has no rider. For this (man) needed the rider which is reason. 90
>
> This is also the way in which he [Jesus] speaks of our mind, as if it were a lamp, which burns and lights up the place. 99 Do not tire of knocking on the door of reason. . . 103
>
> Light the lamp within you. Do not extinguish it. 106

Plus ça change, plus c'est la même chose. (Alphonse Karr 1808–1890. The more things change, the more they remain the same.)

There are many other sources of valuable knowledge that the Fellowship of Reason will seek out, collect, and preserve for our members.

Integrated world view

As previously mentioned, a full-service Christian church offers classes on subjects unrelated to religion, for example, career planning, marriage and family, parenting, finance, and retirement. Although the subject of the classes is not religion as such, the instructor is likely to be a member of the church and sympathetic to its teachings. The teacher will often integrate the content of the course with the beliefs of the church. For example, a seminar on marriage and family in a religious church might include a homily of the type "the family that prays together stays together." An integrated view of the world and of knowledge is important. Reality is a consistent whole and there are no contradictions. People understand the necessity of non-contradiction and consistency on an intuitive level. People want a consistent world view and for this reason find learning in church of value.

For example, a church that holds man to be an evil wretch infected by Original Sin, doomed to suffer in this life, and incapable of happiness in this world, will not teach its adherents that the purpose of life is happiness, that man's mind is efficacious, and that self-esteem is of value. Such a church will teach in its marriage and family class that you are duty-bound to stay with your physically abusive spouse because divorce is a sin, you are wrong to expect happiness from life, you should pray to God and do your duty as defined by the church so that you might be accepted into Heaven after you are dead.

The sermon given during the regular weekly church service often relates to a current event. The sermon will analyze the current event in light of a passage of scripture read earlier in the service. The minister offers an interpretation of the event consistent with the commonly held beliefs. Exactly as in church-sponsored classes, he offers an integrated world view.

For example, in a church that believes that sex is evil, except for the purpose of procreation in the context of marriage, the minister might relate a current event of infidelity and murder as proof of the point. Or a minister might preach that the existence of a cruel disease such as acquired immune deficiency syndrome, AIDS, is God's punishment of homosexuals for violating His law, citing Romans 1:27: "In the same way the men also abandoned natural relations with women and were inflamed with lust for one another. Men committed indecent acts with other men, and received in themselves the due penalty for their perversion."

The Fellowship of Reason rejects the doctrine of Original Sin and the belief that sex is evil. Therefore, in our marriage and family class, we will encourage you to have that physically abusive spouse arrested and to divorce him. We will teach that you are unique, precious, and capable of achieving happiness in this world. If AIDS is mentioned in a sermon, the message will be to practice safe sex.

The important point is that moral instruction is an objective value. Religion does supply moral instruction whatever the deficiencies in the substantive morality. The Fellowship of Reason intends to provide moral instruction. Our morality, based upon reason, is not deficient.

Conclusion

Rational individualists tend to focus critically upon the irrationality and mysticism of religion. Until now, we have not considered what objective value our five billion brethren find in their religions. Upon examination, we have discovered that celebration of life, fellowship, enjoyment of art, moral instruction and learning, regular reorientation with core values, and personal meditation and reflection are indeed objective values that can be achieved in a rational context within the Fellowship of Reason.

In the next chapter we will begin learning about the moral philosophy of the Fellowship of Reason starting with the most important thing in the world.

Chapter 2—The Value of Human Life

Every individual life is infinitely precious.—RonaldReagan, to students at Moscow State University, May 31, 1988

All the nations will be gathered before him, and he will separate the people one from another as a shepherd separates the sheep from the goats. He will put the sheep on his right and the goats on his left. Then the King will say to those on his right, "Come, you who are blessed by my Father; take your inheritance, the kingdom prepared for you since the creation of the world." —Matthew 25:32–34

Then he will say to those on his left, "Depart from me, you who are cursed, into the eternal fire prepared for the devil and his angels." —Matthew 25:41

[The proletarians] have nothing of their own to secure and to fortify; their mission is to destroy all previous securities for, and insurances of, individual property. —Marx 1848

We are not interested in the utility of a particular species, or free-flowing river, or ecosystem, to mankind. They have intrinsic value, more value—to me—than another human body, or a billion of them. Human happiness, and certainly human fecundity, are not as important as a wild and healthy planet.
—Graber 1989, p. 10

No compromise in defense of Mother Earth! Battle cry of Earth First! —www.earthfirstjournal.org

The Fellowship of Reason is a moral community. A moral community is a group of people who are united by a common interest in a particular moral philosophy. Moral communities study and practice ethics. Ethics answers the question "how ought I to live?" To live is to act. Action implies a goal. A particular ethics, then, must have an ultimate goal by which to proscribe rules for action that will answer this question.

We begin by specifying the ultimate value, according to the moral philosophy of the Fellowship of Reason. The ultimate value for us is the individual human being. The goal of the Fellowship of Reason is to foster the successful life and happiness of individual human beings.

It may surprise you that not everyone shares this view.

Different Views

As the quotations at the beginning of the chapter reveal, people value individual human life in varying degrees—some infinitely, like Ronald Reagan, and some, like David M. Graber, less than a river. The western religious view is that God is the highest value and certain human beings, the faithful, are lesser, penultimate values. The unfaithful are damned and of no value. The communistic view is that the proletariat is the highest value to which individual human beings may be sacrificed. For some like the Nazis, a particular race of people is the highest value. The radical environmentalist view is that "mother earth" is more valuable than individual human beings.

Obviously, many people do not take the time to organize their personal value systems and, accordingly, they hold a mixture of these views, never discovering the contradictions implicit in their choices. For example, I imagine one could find a supporter of Earth First!, a radical environmentalist group valuing "mother earth" as ultimate, who also claims to be a Christian. Christianity values God as ultimate and man as penultimate. The contradiction in such a person's value system is illustrated by this passage from the Bible: "Then God said, 'Let us make man in our image, in our likeness, and let them rule over the fish of the sea and the birds of the air, over the livestock, over all the earth, and over all the creatures that move along the ground.'" Genesis 1:26. A member of Earth First! would certainly chafe at God's grant to man of sovereignty over the earth.

One must be clear about his ultimate value if he is to formulate coherent rules to guide his life.

The most fundamental distinguishing characteristic of the moral philosophy embraced by the Fellowship of Reason is that our philosophy regards individual human life as the highest value.

Individual Human Life Is the Ultimate Value

The radiant existent that is you is supremely valuable. Each of us is his own ultimate value. Let me show you why.

Before defining the concept of value, let us consider concepts generally. A particular concept is applicable within a certain context. Take, for example, the concept of color. Color is the human mental experience of a certain wavelength of light acting upon the human eye as interpreted by the human brain. The wavelengths of visible electromagnetic radiation start at about 0.0007 millimeters for red and go to about 0.0004 millimeters for violet. Outside of these wavelengths acting upon the human eye the concept of color does not apply. It does not make sense to talk about the color of X rays which are not visible to the human eye. It does not make sense to talk about the color of justice or the color of love or the color of God or the color of a symphony.

All concepts have a context in which they arise, to which they apply, and within which they are meaningful.

The concept of value, like the concept of color, has a context. Just as the concept color pertains to the relationship between a certain type of electromagnetic radiation and the human eye, so the concept of value pertains to a certain relationship. The concept of value pertains to the relationship between entities that act and the objects of their actions. The only entities that act are living entities.

Here is a definition of value—a value is that which a living entity acts to gain and keep. The novelist Ayn Rand originated this formulation.

A rock cannot value. It is meaningless to say that something is of value to a rock. Inanimate objects have no values. Value is a concept that

35

applies only within the context of living beings. It makes sense to say that sunlight is of value to photosynthetic plants. It makes sense to say that food is of value to animals.

The context of the concept of value is life.

"Life is a process of self-sustaining and self-generated action (Rand 1957, p. 1013)." Living entities are continuously metabolizing, growing, reproducing, and adapting. When a living entity stops acting, it dies. If a living being is to live, it must act. It must act in a certain way. The way it must act is determined by its nature. The goal of its action, if it is to continue to exist, must be its own life.

Value is the concept that identifies this important relationship between entities and the actions of entities.

If a living entity's action furthers its life, then that action is valuable. If a living entity's action threatens its life, then that action is not valuable. Life is the standard of value. All lesser values are judged by the standard of life—for it or against it. Life is the ultimate value.

The context of the concept of value is the action of living beings. The concept of value has no meaning outside of life just like color has no meaning outside the wavelengths of the visible spectrum.

The life each living entity has to live is its own. Therefore, your own life is your own ultimate value.

Human Life Is More than Survival at Any Price

Do not misunderstand me. I am not saying the preservation of your own skin is all there is to the wonder that is you.

Human beings possess a conceptual consciousness. An individual human being is not only concerned with his physical survival, but also with his spiritual survival. Happiness is the conscious human experience of successful living. Happiness is the reward and standard of successful living.

For an individual human being to survive, both body and mind must be considered.

FELLOWSHIP OF REASON

Unlike other living beings, human beings can choose to live or not. In order to maintain the choice to live, a person must experience his life as valuable or as potentially valuable. As you create your life over time, you will accumulate values that are immeasurably precious. Your spouse and your children will top the list. You will have friends who are immensely valuable. You will naturally invest a great deal of the time of your life into the care and well-being of your spouse, your children, and your friends. If tragedy strikes, you may well decide to invest the balance of your life to save your values. That is, you may, in an emergency, spend your life to save a beloved child, spouse, or friend.

You may wonder, how can I be my own ultimate value and still give my life to save my beloved? The answer is that your life is your own creation and it consists of *your* spouse, *your* child, and *your* friend, among other things. A human being's life is a rich tapestry of people and experiences. Human life is not mere survival after the fashion of a mangy dog living out of garbage cans. Human life is work, family, friends, hobbies, art, and physical activity. All of these elements must be present if you are to live a happy life. Once you have created the content of your life, the loss of some component of your life may become unacceptable. You may decide that the best choice for you personally, in order to optimize your happiness, is to spend your entire life in one final act of glory. In extraordinary circumstances, one's happiness may be optimized by choosing his own physical death.

Consider the climax of the popular film *Independence Day* (1996). Aliens have attacked earth. The forces of the human race are on the verge of defeat and the entire population of earth faces annihilation. The character Russell Casse (played by Randy Quaid) is among the pilots engaged in the final air assault upon the alien invaders. This pilot is factually, according to the story, earth's last chance, and he knows it. The only way he can succeed is by smashing his jet fighter into the enemy spaceship, thus destroying the invaders and himself.

Russell Casse's heroic suicide is rational upon the standard of his own life. The pilot is acting in accordance with his values at the cost of his life. He is "spending" his life for his values.

First of all, it is apparent that the pilot's life, his ultimate value, is forfeit in either case. He will die instantly by crashing into the spaceship or in a few days when the aliens clean up the few remaining human survivors. If he acts to destroy the aliens, he will save his children from certain death. The pilot's children are, factually, his penultimate values. By killing the aliens, he achieves his penultimate values, his children's lives. By killing the aliens, the pilot will preserve earth and humanity, which will be of value to his surviving children. The pilot will derive great personal satisfaction by killing an enemy who had inflicted a personal injustice and physical injury upon him (years previously the aliens had kidnapped him). It is clear that by killing the enemy (and losing his life), the pilot will achieve many of his own values. As a secondary consequence, the pilot's action benefits all of surviving humankind.

If the pilot had chosen self-preservation, he would have been able to watch from the air while his children and the rest of humanity were destroyed. He himself would have shortly suffered annihilation. Awaiting his certain death, he would suffer a sense of great guilt for not having acted with integrity to sustain his values.

I intend by citing this example from *Independence Day* to clarify a common confusion. People sometimes equate a rational individualist with a "selfish" person. By convention, a "selfish" person is one who by word or deed declares that he does not recognize the value of other individuals. The hero in this example acts rationally to achieve his own interests—his honor, his children, and justice—even though he dies. To a rational individualist, he and other individuals are the source of all values. A truly "selfish" person who did not recognize the value of others would, as a consequence of his lack of virtue, deprive himself of human psychological visibility and all economic trade. He would become a hermit in a cave, if he survived at all. A rational individualist does not deny the value of individual human beings. He recognizes that individual human beings are the fountainheads of all values.

FELLOWSHIP OF REASON

THERE ARE NO CONFLICTS OF INTEREST AMONG RATIONAL MEN

If individual human beings are the source of all values, it follows that cooperation, rather than conflict, is the rational method of operation.

A common misconception about the nature of man is that human beings are like a school of sharks in a feeding frenzy fighting over a bloody carcass. Another, more human image comes to mind—customers at a department store clearance sale fighting over the low-priced markdown items.

These images do not capture the essential nature of man, the rational individualist. Of course, some men do behave like murderous beasts. But rational individualists who live by a certain principle (the trader principle) do not sink to these sub-human levels.

In discovering the true nature of man, the most important fact to note is that the products and services necessary for human life are not just "out there" in the world waiting for the aggressive shark or bargain-hunting shopper to find them. The products and services necessary for human life are created every day by productive men and women. The creation of these products and services requires two conditions: (1) the mental and physical effort of the individual producers; and (2) a society that respects individual rights.

Producers cannot produce if their time is spent defending their product from looters and thieves (sharks). Bill Gates and Microsoft Corporation come to mind. At this writing (2000) Microsoft is in the midst of antitrust litigation. The productive time of many employees and huge monetary resources of Microsoft are being diverted from that which Microsoft has done best—building and operating one of the greatest computer software companies ever.

Man's rational nature is a trader. A trader is a producer who exchanges his values in voluntary transactions with others for the products and services he desires. This can only happen in a society where men are free and property rights are protected.

It is not in man's rational interest to live in a dog-eat-dog society. And the trader relationship is not a dog-eat-dog relationship. In a voluntary

39

trade, both parties win. When I trade the dollar in my pocket for the soft drink in the fast-food store at the corner, we both get what we want. I get the soft drink I wanted to quench my thirst. The store owner gets the dollar he wanted.

A dog-eat-dog society is one in which people do not deal with one another by voluntary trade, but by force. That force can be open warfare, crime, fraud, or government action.

The rational individualist respects the rights of all other people. He expects his rights to be respected. He recognizes himself as his own ultimate value. He recognizes that everyone else is his own ultimate value. He expects to deal with others only in voluntary transactions, only when the others freely choose to deal with him.

If a man accepts that his interests are best served in a society based upon free and voluntary trade (and a rational individualist does), then the interests of the individual are identical with those of all other individuals.

Stated another way, the assertion that "there are no conflicts of interest among rational men" means that if a person accepts the proposition that force is irrational and that all relationships among people should and shall be voluntary, then there are no conflicts of interest among such people. So, for example, take the case of two men in love with the same woman. One might say, on a superficial level, that there is a conflict of interest between the men. But, if the woman's judgment in the matter is important to both men (and it will be to rational men), both men will have the desire that the woman choose the man she loves. It is true that each man might dream of a different reality—one in which he is the beloved—but that is a conflict with reality, not with the other man.

To revisit the shopping frenzy example briefly, it is possible for one person to create circumstances where values are obtained in regulated physical contests. Boxing, wrestling, and football are examples. The participants voluntarily participate. When a department store sets up a sale in which the low-priced merchandise goes to the quickest or the strongest, the shoppers' decision to participate in the melee is voluntary.

FELLOWSHIP OF REASON

HISTORICAL CONSEQUENCES OF OTHER VIEWS

It is interesting to note the historical consequences of the different views of the value of individual human life—the religious, the statist, and the environmental. In the religious view, God is the ultimate value. Throughout history theists have condoned and conducted persecutions of and wars against all of those who were not among God's chosen people. Witness the Old Testament, the Crusades, and the Inquisition. In the statist view, some group is the ultimate value. Advocates of these value systems ultimately value the state, the party, the proletariat, the poor, the majority, or the race. In the course of the twentieth century, the social system called communism killed over 100 million people. Do not imagine that these social systems were of good intention and just taken over by bad men. In any system in which individual human life is not the ultimate value, you will find individual human beings paying with their lives and property for the "higher" values of the system as determined by the masters of the system, be they priests, kings, committees, congresses, parliaments, or dictators. Examples of such individuals sacrificed to a "higher" good include the 20 million people murdered by Stalin in the USSR, the 6.3 million Jews murdered by Hitler in the Holocaust, the 65 million Chinese murdered by Mao, and the 2 million people of Cambodia murdered by Pol Pot. For full details of the death toll in the twentieth century, see *The Black Book of Communism: Crimes, Terror, Repression* (1999).

Fortunately, the radical environmentalist movement is so marginal that it has not accumulated many human victims, though in principle it might. Tom Clancy's novel *Rainbow Six* (1998) explores the theme of environmentalism gone mad. In the book a group of eco-terrorists inoculate themselves and conspire to kill the rest of humanity with a lethal virus in order to save "mother earth" from man.

OURS IS A PHILOSOPHY FOR LIVING ON EARTH

Let me be crystal clear about this point. For theists, God is the ultimate value. Because he is the ultimate value, individual human beings can be the unwilling means to the ends of God as interpreted by God's self-

41

proclaimed agents on earth. To be an unwilling means to another's end implies that you can be expropriated, enslaved, tortured, or killed in accordance with the whim of the authoritative interpreters of God's will. In the history of religion, this is precisely what has happened—from the cruel sacrifice of living human beings to the gods of primitive cultures, to any "holy" war you care to mention. People are sacrificed to theists' ultimate value—God.

For statist value systems, the party, the proletariat, the poor, the majority, or the race is the ultimate value. Because some group is the ultimate value, individual human beings can be the unwilling means to the ends of that group. You can be expropriated, enslaved, tortured, or killed in accordance with the whim of the authoritative interpreters of the will of the group, be that Stalin, Hitler, Mao, Pol Pot, or bureaucratic bean counters. People are sacrificed to the statist's ultimate value—the group.

For rational individualists, individual human life is sacred and inviolable. Other people, according to our philosophy of reason, should never be unwilling means to another's ends. There will be no human sacrifices to a god, or the group, or "mother earth" in a world committed to our philosophy of reason. Each of us has the moral right to live for himself.

Now, I trust, my point is clear. Theism, statism, and radical environmentalism do not value life. Rational individualism does. If you define the good as productive of life and the bad as productive of human corpses, your choice is made obvious.

We have learned that the ultimate value is individual human life. In the next chapter we will discover the meaning of life and how to achieve happiness.

Chapter 3—What is the Meaning of Your Life?

People say that what we're all seeking is a meaning for life. I don't think that's what we're really seeking. I think that what we're seeking is an experience of being alive, so that our life experiences on the purely physical plane will have resonances within our own innermost being and reality, so that we actually feel the rapture of being alive. —Campbell 1991, p. 4, 5

"Meaningless! Meaningless!" says the Teacher. "Utterly meaningless! Everything is meaningless."—Ecclesiastes 1:2

Thus, in essence, what our life is consists in experiences related to work, to keeping things we already have from falling apart, and to whatever else we do in our free time. It is within these parameters that life unfolds, and it is how we choose what we do, and how we approach it, that will determine whether the sum of our days adds up to a formless blur, or to something resembling a work of art. —Csikszentmihalyi 1997, p. 13

My friend, suffering his mid-life crisis, filed for divorce from his wife of fifteen years. They have two children, ages six and four, for whose psychological health I fear. He sent me an e-mail at webmaster@kindreason.com, the website of the Atlanta chapter of the Fellowship of Reason, asking for help. I took that opportunity to respond to him in my capacity as the director of a moral community and as his friend. I e-mailed him a longish essay suggesting that he faced a *crisis of meaning* and that he should ask himself who he really wants to be and to become that person—advice as old as antiquity. (The Oracle at Delphi advised, "Know thyself.") I had no opinion about whether he should or should not proceed with the divorce. He wrote back that he had "scanned" the essay, that he did not have time to read it, and that I had obviously talked with his wife (which I had not). He told my wife later that he did not read my essay because he thought that it was some kind of "religious diatribe." The words "morality" and "virtue" appeared in the writing.

If his reaction were not so tragic, one might be tempted to laugh. The Fellowship of Reason cannot be mistaken for a religious organization.

His decision not to read my essay, because he spied the words "morality" and "virtue" upon a cursory glance, has deep cultural roots and evidences a common cultural problem.

Morality and virtue, as commonly preached in our culture, are tiresome at best, and inimical to human life and happiness at worst. Many people regard "morality" as a code word requiring them to give up what they truly want for the benefit of somebody for whom they care not one iota. "Virtue" means, simply, celibacy to many people. In our culture morality and virtue have a bad reputation. I blame the morality of religion, the goal of which is not happiness on earth, but an undefined post-mortem bliss.

In the Fellowship of Reason individuals use morality to achieve their lives and happiness on earth. Our morality does not require you to give up your earthly values for a heavenly reward beyond the grave. Our morality shows you how to acquire your values in this life. Virtue has nothing to do with celibacy. Human sexuality is wondrously good. Virtues are necessary character traits for achieving your own life and happiness.

My friend suffers from a crisis of meaning. Only careful thought about the meaning of his life can save him and his children. In our morality rational thought is the primary virtue. Because I used the words "morality" and "virtue" to advise him—words poisoned by the otherworldly morality of religion—my friend would not hear me.

My friend is suffering from a crisis of meaning. He does not know the meaning of his life. But what is the meaning of life?

FELLOWSHIP OF REASON

Not "What Is the Meaning of Life?" But "What Is the Meaning of My Life?"

Life is an end in itself. For any living being, its own proper end or goal is right function in accordance with its nature. But an individual need not ask, "what is the meaning of life, in general?" That is a question for philosophers. Rather, he or she needs to ask "what will be the meaning of my life and how will I achieve that meaning?" For an individual this is the relevant question. Each individual's answer to the question will be unique. Because each individual's answer is unique, discovering the meaning of his life will be hard, important work. The Fellowship of Reason helps individuals with this crucial task.

Life and Happiness

I demonstrated in chapter 2 that the ultimate end of the action of any individual organism was its own life. That proposition is true for human beings, too. Human beings are a unified organism of mind and body. Unlike other living things, human beings have a conceptual consciousness. The manifestation in human consciousness of the active and successful exercise of all of the faculties of the individual is happiness. Note that the verb "to happen" and the noun "happiness" come from the same Middle English root, *hap*. If one's life is "happening" well, if he has well being, then he is happy.

Health and happiness are the physical and psychological manifestations in a human being of a singular process—life. For man, happiness is an end in itself. Happiness, well being, or right functioning in accordance with man's nature is the purpose of life. Happiness or the potential for happiness is the reason human beings live.

A man in love looking into the eyes of his beloved does not ask, "What is the meaning of life?" He knows. A woman nursing her newborn baby does not ask it. She knows. An artist in the midst of creative ecstasy does not ask it either. He or she knows.

The meaning of your life is in your experience of it. In the words of Joseph Campbell, it is a deep experience of being alive. The crucial task of each individual is to find those activities and to achieve those conditions that bring the deepest experiences of being alive.

Three Senses of Meaning

The word "meaning" has at least three senses: (1) Meaning can be used in the sense of the goal or purpose of something. For example, why is he going to law school? What is the meaning (goal or purpose) of going to law school? Is he going into business, will he enter private practice, or is he a professional student? (2) Meaning can be used in the sense of a person's intention. For example, why did he walk out like that? What does he mean (intend) by leaving without saying goodbye? (3) Meaning can be used in the sense of the definition of something. For example, what is the meaning (definition) of the word "magazine"? A magazine is a publication, usually in paperback, containing articles and stories, and often pictures and illustrations, which appears at regular intervals.

Let us consider the question "what is the *meaning* of my life" utilizing each of these three senses of meaning.

What is the meaning (*goal or purpose*) of my life? When a person decides to create and successfully operate a new entrepreneurial business, that person has a challenging goal for his life. We have a sense that Ted Turner's creation of CNN is a worthy lifetime achievement. The life of a person who has created a successful business has meaning.

What is the meaning (*intention*) of my life? A person can have a stated goal. But that is not enough. She must *intend* to achieve her purpose. If a person's stated goal is to have happy, healthy children, but she takes no action to locate a suitable life-mate to help in the creation and raising of those hoped-for children, then we might fairly question her intentions. If, on the other hand, she applies all of her skills of mind and body to the task, then we might well say that she intends to have a family.

What is the meaning (*definition*) of my life? The actual activities that a person performs each day define his existence. You are what you do.

The life of a person with self-selected goals for his life, who has the intention of carrying out his chosen purposes, and who acts out his intentions and thus defines his daily life in terms of his self-selected goals, has meaning in all three senses of the word—goal or purpose, intention, and definition.

Notice that everyone's life has "meaning" in the sense of definition. Not everyone has a stated goal or purpose. Some who have a stated goal or purpose have no intention of carrying it out, as evidenced by their inactivity. Shortly, we will learn the actual meaning of your life in the sense of definition. The Fellowship of Reason advocates that everyone should have meaning in their life in the sense of a long-range goal or purpose and in the sense of an actual intention (evidenced by action) of carrying that goal or purpose to conclusion.

The specific actions that an individual takes to achieve his life *is* the meaning of his life. If an individual's actions are consciously chosen according to a master goal or purpose, the sum of his days will resemble a work of art. If an individual's actions are determined by the circumstances of the moment with no reference to long-range goals or purposes, the sum of his days will resemble a formless blur.

Let us proceed to discover our present meaning, in the sense of definition. How do we actually live our days now?

What Is the Meaning of Your Life Today?

Our goals in this section are (1) to determine the meaning (*definition*) of our lives implied by our actual activities, (2) to evaluate that meaning, and (3) to consider whether any changes are in order.

By way of excuse for myself (and perhaps others) for having a life more resembling a formless blur than a work of art, let me make these observations. It is not easy to start from scratch, as an abstract intellectual exercise, and set goals for our lives. Many young people do not start out their adulthood by asking and answering questions like these: Where will I live? What will I do for a living? Will I get married? Will I have children?

Many young people, having absorbed the expectations of their family and culture, simply proceed to fulfill the expectations of others. Only years later, if ever, do they consider that another, better path was available to them.

Some young people make important decisions on the spur of the moment and without serious consideration. A boy falls in love so he gets married. A young girl thinks it's cool to have sex so she does. She gets pregnant and births a baby that she is psychologically and economically unable to raise. A young woman is offered a high-paying job outside her field of interest. She goes for the money.

There are problems with making important decisions on the spur of the moment. Falling in love is wonderful, but if there are fundamental value differences, for example, differences of deep religious conviction, powerful sexual attraction alone will not make for long-term marital happiness. Having children without serious consideration of the twenty-year commitment involved is an injustice to the couple and the unborn child. Taking a job for money alone without considering whether one's days will be filled with happiness or drudgery is not the best way to achieve happiness in this life.

It is possible, though, to set your life goals and then proceed to achieve them at any stage of life. In youth, setting your life goals is both easier and harder. It is easier because you have few irrevocable commitments in youth. You are not married. You do not have children. You do not have many years invested in a job with only a few years remaining to earn your retirement. It is harder because as a young person you may not have had the experience necessary to learn what exactly it is that you wish to do with your life.

For most of us, it is impractical to consider our life goals abstractly, because we do have irrevocable commitments. The adventure of parenting is an irrevocable commitment. All life planning of parents must include provisions for the care and nurturing of their children. The adventure of marriage is a commitment not easily withdrawn. All life planning of marital partners should be made in the context of the marriage partnership. If one has only four years left to earn a lifetime pension after sixteen or more years of hard work, most of us would likely tough it out rather than change careers at such a time.

For the mature adult who has already made irrevocable choices, life planning cannot be an abstract mental exercise. Another, more practical approach is indicated. One approach is to take an inventory of his or her present life and evaluate it.

Let us take that inventory now. The numbers used in the specific inventory that follows will be different from your own personal circumstances, but this example will illustrate how you can perform your own personal inventory of the implicit meaning of your life.

LIFE "TIME" INVENTORY

The question we are considering is how do we *actually* spend the time of our lives. We will use this inventory to determine the implicit meaning (*definition*) of our lives now. Then we will evaluate that implicit meaning, identify imbalances, and consider whether changes are necessary.

We will base our inventory upon an entire week of time upon the assumption that one average week contains almost all of the usual elements of our lives. Annual vacations and holidays are not usual events of a typical week and will therefore not be counted in this inventory. Nevertheless, both vacations and holidays have an important place in a full life.

There are 168 hours to live in a week.

Sleep

Our inventory begins with sleep. We sleep every day. Most people sleep for at least 8 hours

We are left with 112 waking hours to live each week.

Personal maintenance

We spend time attending to personal hygiene and maintenance each week. Activities such as showering, shaving, going to the bathroom, and eating are included in this category. These activities consume about 2½ hours of time each day.

We are left with 94½ hours to live each week.

Career

Most of us spend at least eight hours per day, five days per week working at our careers. Most of us work away from home and therefore

49

have to commute. Let us say for the purposes of this hypothetical life "time" inventory that commuting takes one hour per day. Career and commuting consume the single largest block of the time of our precious lives, about 45 hours per week.

Our work is a very important element in defining the meaning of our lives. We devote the next chapter to a discussion of this crucial category. When we create our statement of the purpose of our lives, work will play a central role.

We are left with 49½ hours to live each week.

Television

On average, Americans and Canadians watch about three hours of television per day. That is a total of 21 hours per week.

Note that if you watch this much television, you are spending about 42% of your non-career life watching television. An able-bodied person who watches this much television is wasting his life. Television is like alcohol, drugs, and gambling. Each has its legitimate uses. None are evil *per se*. But all can be abused. Use of television at such high levels suggests that it is being used as a stress reliever. Rather than sedation through television, a television abuser should seek out the cause of his stress and eliminate it.

Excessive television viewing is the first place to cut down in order to enhance the quality of our lives.

The proper amount of your life to spend watching television is, like each of the decisions in this inventory, completely personal. Let us say that 10 hours per week, including watching rented videos, is a reasonable amount of television per week.

We had 49½ hours remaining from the previous section. Television takes 10 hours. We are left with 39½ hours to live each week.

Health and fitness

Many enjoy and are capable of participating in physical activities. Some examples are jogging, weightlifting, and sailing. Unlike television, we are likely to spend too little time in these activities. Our bodies are designed to give us pleasure. If we fail to use them, they will atrophy and

FELLOWSHIP OF REASON

become diseased. If we want to live many more years, we will have to maintain our bodies by using them well. Let us say that eight hours per week is a reasonable amount of time to devote to personal health and fitness.

We are left with 31½ hours to live each week.

Art, music, and reading

Art has an especially important place in the life of human beings. Because we do "set high and noble goals and perish in pursuit of them," human beings need occasional respite from our efforts during which we can experience the sense of living in our hoped-for, worked-for world. The enjoyment of art allows a person with long-range, lifetime goals to recharge his batteries so that he can continue his life's work with renewed hope and vigor.

Understanding that art gives us hope and vigor to live on helps to explain our desire for happy endings in fiction. A happy ending suggests a world where human action is rewarded by success, where happiness is man's natural, to-be-expected state. Unhappy art does not imbue a person with hope and vigor.

Perhaps the most accessible forms of art are books and music. But all of the arts—architecture, dance, drama, literature, music, painting, poetry, and sculpture—can express the sense of life that mirrors one's own.

Let us say that 10 hours per week is an appropriate length of time to give to the activity of enjoying art, music, and reading.

We are left with 21½ hours to live each week.

Self-improvement and hobbies

None of us is perfect. We are all works in progress. We need to reserve time to work on our most important project—ourselves. Reading self-improvement books, studying and learning new things, practicing the piano, and exercising are all activities that fall in this category. While there is overlap with other categories, self-improvement is important enough to merit special emphasis.

Let us say that thirty minutes per day should be dedicated to this important activity.

We are left with 18 hours to live each week.

Friends

Mihaly Csikszentmihalyi, author of *Flow: The Psychology of Optimal Experience*, writes: "[F]riendships rarely happen by chance: one must cultivate them as assiduously as one must cultivate a job or a family (1991, p. 190)."

Friends are important for personal psychological visibility. In a friend, we experience our values personified in our friend's character. In friends, we experience the value that is ourselves made evident by their interaction with us.

Rarely do we think about working on our friendships. Considering the importance they naturally have, that fact is surprising. We need to call our friends, to have dinner with our friends, and to celebrate with our friends.

I suggest that at least four hours per week should be given to nurturing our friendships.

We are left with 14 hours to live each week.

Marriage

Intimate relationships give us the greatest pleasure and are the most important relationships in our lives. Often there is only one intimate relationship in a person's life and that relationship is with a spouse.

Intimate relationships require the most attention of all of the activities of your life.

I suggest that at least four hours per week, about half an hour per day, should be dedicated exclusively to caring for and attending to your intimate relationship. This time is over and above the time spent together sleeping, eating, and watching television, for example.

We are left with 10 hours to live each week.

Children

Parenting is the most important job in the world. It is also the most underappreciated. There is almost no formal education in parenting skills.

This failure of educational institutions presents an incredible opportunity for the Fellowship of Reason.

The choice to have children is one of the three most important commitments a person can make. As mentioned previously, career and marriage are the other two. If you choose to have children, they will be quite demanding of your time and attention. Infants and toddlers require constant, loving care. Only when children start school are the demands somewhat reduced, but only by the amount of time they are actually at school.

The project of raising children will last at least 18 years.

Given these considerations it is impossible to number the hours in a week dedicated to raising a child. *Every* hour is dedicated to your child. Your child is an omnipresent part of your life. You will eat, sleep, and work with the child close at hand.

Spiritual exercise

An entire chapter of this book is devoted to the subject of spiritual exercise. Briefly, spiritual exercise is a written self-dialog or a conversation with another for the purpose of moving yourself closer to joy by dealing with past guilt, future fear, or a current problem.

As rational individualists we need to clean up and clear out the debris in our minds. After all, our goal is personal happiness. We all hope to live without pain or fear or guilt. To achieve that state of radiant joy we now only read about in fiction, we must actively ferret out pain and fear and guilt from our souls.

Five hours per week is appropriate for spiritual exercise. We had 10 hours remaining from the previous section. We are left with 5 hours to live each week.

Planning

You should monitor your life for success and progress. You need to monitor your activities in light of the stated purpose of your life. We will learn how to make the definitive statement of the purpose of our lives in the next chapter. We need to update our life "time" inventory regularly and to evaluate it. We need to make sure that we are saving for long-term needs like retirement and health care. We need to make sure we are addressing all of our long-range goals on a weekly basis.

The Fellowship of Reason meets weekly for one hour. With commuting, socializing, and attending the meeting, our remaining 5 hours are just enough to allow for this important activity.

Summary of time inventory

We have identified the following categories of the activities of your life:
- Sleep
- Personal maintenance
- Career
- Television
- Health and fitness
- Art, music, and reading
- Self-improvement and hobbies
- Friends
- Marriage
- Children
- Spiritual exercise
- Planning

If you perform this inventory, you will know how you currently spend the time of your life. You will have identified the implicit meaning (*definition*) of your life. What do you think? At the end of your days, will you look back with pride and contentment on such a life?

EVALUATION OF LIFE "TIME" INVENTORY

Let us proceed to evaluate your life "time" inventory.

Your days are numbered

We are undertaking this evaluation of the time of our lives because our days are numbered. Because our days are numbered, they are valuable and should be cherished.

In performing a life "time" inventory you will have actually numbered the hours of your week. Let us make an estimate of how many days and hours you have remaining to live so that we can appreciate just how dear those days and hours are.

To make an estimate of your remaining lifespan, consider how long your parents, grandparents, or great-grandparents lived. Using ancestor longevity as a standard, pick a likely age for your own demise. Take your own present age, subtract your present age from the age of your predicted end, and multiply that number by 365. The product is an estimate of the number of days that you have remaining to live.

For example, at this writing I am 46 years old. My father died when he was 74. The difference between 74 and 46 is 28. Assuming I have the same longevity as my father, I have 10,220 days to live. This number may seem large, but I have lived 10,220 days as an adult since I was 18 years old. I remember those 10,220 days. I can put that span of time in my mind. Looking back, it does not seem very long.

With that period of time in mind, both looking forward and looking backward, I am in a better position to evaluate how I have spent my life and how I will spend it in the future. As an example of the evaluation process, let us evaluate how I might spend a part of my remaining lifespan.

I have said that I may have 10,220 days left to live. That is equivalent to 245,280 total hours to live. After deducting sleeping hours, I have 163,520 waking hours to live. After taking out time for personal maintenance (25,550 hours) and career (65,520 hours), I have 72,450 to live.

Suppose I find myself 28 years from now at age 74 looking back on my 72,450 hours after sleep, personal maintenance, and career since I was 46. Suppose further that I was an average American or Canadian and had spent 21 hours per week watching television to relieve work-related stress for the last 28 years. I take out my calculator and compute that I have spent 30,576 hours of that time watching television. I will have spent over 42% of the precious time of my life, after sleep, personal maintenance, and career, watching television. I try to imagine what that 42% has added up to. I realize that I used that precious time of my life to make it possible to tolerate the stress of a career I have hated. Oops! Time is up. My life is over.

I can with a certain mathematical precision produce a negative evaluation of using television to relieve the psychic pain of a poor career choice. I will be motivated by this knowledge to change careers and to modify my television viewing habits.

Imbalances

In order to avoid such personal tragedy (discovering at the end of your life that you have wasted all or a significant portion of your life), you *must* evaluate the things that you do every day now. You *must* look at your life and determine if there are significant imbalances among the important categories of your life's activities. Those categories include sleep, personal maintenance, career, television, health and fitness, art, self-improvement and hobbies, friends, marriage, children, spiritual exercise, planning, and holidays.

If you have the courage to take a life "time" inventory, it is likely that you will find some misspent time. I have mentioned television abuse. The couch potatoes among us are on notice of a possible imbalance.

Here is a similar problem. If a person finds in his life "time" inventory that he spends hours every day consuming a twelve-pack of beer, then falls asleep for the night and awakens the next morning with a hangover, he is on notice of another imbalance. If a person is going to spend the balance of his non-career, waking hours in the semi-conscious fog of intoxication, it is time to start praying for an afterlife. It is certain that such a person's earthly life (there is no other) will not count for much in his own eyes.

Other symptoms of a life imbalance include drug abuse, eating disorders, obesity, compulsive gambling, spousal and child abuse, excessive sleep, depression, chronic stress, and chronic illness. The presence of any of these symptoms in the life "time" inventory indicates the need for professional assistance.

Don't waste time

You must not waste a minute of the precious time of your life on activities you do not enjoy.

If you have a poker club or acquaintance or job that has come to bore or annoy you, you ought to quit it or him. You should not perform an unhappy task merely to spare the feelings of friends or family or employer. You ought to live your own life honestly. You ought not to live someone else's expectations for your own life. You need not be rude or unpleasant. You can resign or decline gracefully, but do resign or decline.

Once you have eliminated activities that do not serve your own expectations for your life, you may find that there is more room for pleasurable activities to which you have devoted too little time. For example, you may find that you have more time to cultivate friendships or more time to pursue your hobbies. You may also discover that television abuse is no longer necessary to your sanity, as did I.

These are personal choices

Let me emphasize that the choices of the activities of a person's life are personal choices. The choices of a particular career, physical fitness routine, art, friends, self-improvement and hobbies, and holidays are all morally optional. A person is morally obligated to make these choices consciously. A person is morally obligated to make these choices upon the standard of his own happiness. A person is morally obligated to choose his own happiness and not to live his life for other people or in accordance with the expectations of other people.

The moral penalty one pays for acting otherwise is not the moral disapprobation of others. The penalty one pays for immoral choices is his own unhappiness. The individual's reward for moral choices is his own happiness.

Also let me clarify that I do not say that a person must have a marriage or children in order to be happy. I do claim that he must have intimate friendships to be happy. I do not say that a person should not watch television. I do claim that he should not use television regularly as a sedative to relieve work-related stress or as a balm for depression. I do not say that a person must enjoy the symphony. I do claim that he must find a form of art—books or films, for example—that gives him the pleasure of seeing his own sense of life made real.

Filling the precious time of your life is a personal task. There is no one to tell you that you have lived your life well. Not many care. But *you* should care. It is your life to live well or not.

Heed the advice of Mihaly Csikszentmihalyi: "[A] joyful life is an individual creation that cannot be copied from a recipe (1991, p. xi)."

Is your life as presently defined rewarding you with happiness, with deep experiences of being alive? In the next chapter we will learn how to discover your own personal destiny, which, if realized, is guaranteed to bring you joy.

Chapter 4—Your Personal Destiny

Many people feel that the time they spend at work is essentially wasted—they are alienated from it, and the psychic energy invested in the job does nothing to strengthen their self. For quite a few people free time is also wasted. Leisure provides a relaxing respite from work, but it generally consists of passively absorbing information, without using any skills or exploring new opportunities for action. As a result life passes in a sequence of boring and anxious experiences over which a person has little control.   —Csikszentmihalyi 1991, p. 68–69

A sacred burden is this life ye bear; look on it; lift it; bear it solemnly; fail not for sorrow; falter not for sin; but onward, upward, till the goal ye win.   —Frances Ann Kemble

For what purpose humanity is there should not even concern us. Why *you* are there, *that* you should ask yourself. And, if you have no ready answer, then set for yourself goals, high and noble goals, and perish in pursuit of them! I know of no better life purpose than to perish in attempting the great and the impossible.   —Friedrich Nietzsche (1844–1900)

Know thyself.   —The Oracle at Delphi

Become who you are.   —Seneca

In the last chapter you discovered the meaning of your life in the sense of definition. In this chapter we are going to discover how to create a meaning for your life in the sense of long-range goal or purpose.

You Won the Lottery!

Imagine that! You won the lottery. And we are not talking about a measly 1 million dollar lottery. We are talking about the big game, the 60 million dollar lottery. So that rather than a mere $50,000 per year for twenty years, we are talking about $2,000,000 per year for thirty years. You are rich beyond your wildest dreams!

Now imagine what you would do with that kind of money. During the first year, you would pay off all your debts. You would buy houses in the Swiss Alps and the Florida Keys and on the French Riviera. You would have condos overlooking Central Park in New York City and the Champs-Elysées in Paris. You would spend the fall in New York, the winter in the Keys and Switzerland, the spring in Paris, and the summer on the Riviera. You would provide money for Ivy League educations for your children and your nieces and nephews. You would dine in the finest restaurants. You would dress in the finest clothes, attending fabulous parties. If you were not married, you would have many romantic adventures with the most beautiful people in the world.

Now, having done all that, what are you going to do when you get up in the morning (assuming you get up before noon, of course)? Think about it. Be specific. Are you going to read all the great books? Are you going to study a foreign language? Are you going to manage your money? Are you going to adopt or have kids and nurture them to adulthood? Are you going to fight for freedom by actively supporting the Cato Institute? Are you going to found a new magazine? Are you going to open a restaurant? The list goes on forever. You get the idea.

Imagining you have won the lottery is a spiritual exercise. In this exercise, you have imagined that you have solved the problem of survival by winning a huge monetary reward. Next, you have imagined that you have satisfied all of your bodily needs fabulously. Food, shelter, clothing, sex, and recreation are available in their finest and most abundant forms. Finally, you have imagined that your family is showered with your bounty as well. What remains is the thing that you want to do because it has meaning for you, because it is somehow important to you. It is that thing that you should be doing now.

Come back to reality. You have not won the lottery. But if you actually did the imagining just described, you have learned something very important about yourself. You have very likely identified your personal destiny, your personal mission in life.

The odds are against your winning the lottery. The time of your life is limited. So do not waste your time hoping you will. You only have one life in which to do that which is important for you to do. You will have food, shelter, clothing, sex, and recreation in moderation. Your extended family will survive and flourish without your beneficence. Do not wait for the lottery to start living your life. Live it now.

Take the knowledge you have learned from this exercise and consider how you might move toward your personal destiny now. If you imagined that you might read all the great books, then you are in luck. It costs nothing. All the great books are available for free in the public library. All you have to do is arrange your life to make time for fulfilling your personal mission. If you imagined that you would open a restaurant, again you are in luck. You can start learning about the restaurant business by getting a job as a waiter. Learning from the inside is the surest way to succeed in the restaurant business. As a lottery winner, had you just opened a restaurant without knowing the business from the inside out, you would not have succeeded. If you imagined that you would nurture your kids to adulthood, again you are in luck. Having kids is the easiest thing on earth. Almost everybody does it. And there are many precious children available for adoption.

It is not hard to live your personal destiny. It is hard to take the time to identify your personal destiny and to have the courage to live it.

THE PROBLEM OF SURVIVAL AND THE PROBLEM OF MEANING

There are two big problems in life. One is the problem of survival. The other is the problem of meaning. The problem of survival is the problem of providing adequate food, shelter, clothing, sex, and recreation for yourself and your immediate family. In America in the twenty-first century the problem of survival is solved for all able-bodied adults. How? Get a job.

I do not mean to be flippant. I realize that many people have struggled finding work in difficult economic times. But at this writing we are enjoying the best of economic times in America. Many jobs currently go unfilled. Only individuals who have no virtues, who lack even the rudimentary virtues such as personal hygiene, honesty, civility, and punctuality, will go without employment in the present economy. In this book we are concerned with people who have at least those rudimentary virtues and who have as a lifetime goal personal moral progress toward perfect virtue.

For most people, the problem of meaning is *the* problem of adult life in the twenty-first century.

The two problems must not, however, be solved independently.

As an adult, you should first discover your personal destiny. When you know it, then solve the problem of survival *as the way to* solve the problem of meaning. In other words, if your personal destiny is to become a cattle farmer, do not get a job in New York City. Move to Texas and get a job on a cattle ranch. If your personal destiny is to become an actor on Broadway, do not become a waitress in Sparta, Georgia. Become a waitress in New York City and take acting classes during the day.

Your solution to your problem of survival should take you in the direction of solving your problem of meaning.

More Clues to Your Personal Mission in Life

Mythologist Joseph Campbell suggests that you follow your bliss in determining the course of your life. Do that which you love doing. Do what you are passionate about. Some people know their own passion from an early age. Other people do not know what they want to do with their lives. For those to whom the future is not clear, the following techniques of self-discovery are suggested.

Who are your heroes?

First, who are your heroes? Who do you admire? Among the living, I admire the executive director and founder of a certain philosophic institution that promotes our philosophy of reason. My hero created this institution from nothing, starting in his basement, and he has caused it to flourish. He has made significant contributions to our philosophy of reason. The organization is enriching the lives of rational individualists by hosting an annual summer conference offering many interesting speakers and providing wonderful opportunities for fellowship among rational individualists. He is a fine public speaker who excels in understanding his questioners, answering them with clarity and kindness.

Knowing who one of my heroes is allows me to make certain inferences about myself: I value the creation of an institution advancing our philosophy of reason. I value public speaking skills. I value being able to understand my interrogators and being able to respond to them effectively and courteously. I value making intellectual contributions to our philosophy of reason.

Explicitly identifying one of my heroes has been useful to me in determining one of my personal missions in life—the creation of the Fellowship of Reason.

What are your hobbies?

Next, what are your hobbies? What do you enjoy doing in your spare time? Your hobbies are a very strong indicator of where your bliss lies. I have a friend who enjoys visiting and talking with senior citizens. She has a job completely unrelated to her hobby. She has recently started a business in which she videotapes conversations with her elderly clients. She creates an oral history of the client's life for the client and his family.

Another friend was an industrial arts teacher in the public school system for years. He enjoyed woodworking as a hobby. He has since resigned his teaching job and gone into woodworking full time. He has a large shop in which he makes furniture for clients. He operates a school adjacent to his shop in which he teaches woodworking skills. He tours the Southeast giving lectures and conducting woodworking demonstrations.

What was your favorite subject in school?

Your major subject in school is often chosen because it interested you and you were good at it. Use your major as a clue to where your bliss lies.

I was a math major in college because I enjoyed it and because I was good at it. Although I went to law school and am now studying philosophy, the logical rigor of mathematics provided crucial training for both philosophy and law. Perhaps you will find a clue to your personal destiny in your major subject.

What do you enjoy reading?
What do you enjoy reading? As an indicator of personal interests, your personal non-fiction reading choices are excellent. If, for example, you find yourself reading computer and Internet magazines, you might enjoy a career as a webmaster. If you are consumed with a passion for personal finance and the stock market, a job in the securities field might be rewarding.

What are your pipe dreams?
What are your pipe dreams? During moments of leisure, what do you imagine yourself doing? My dream is to be standing on a stage in front of thousands of people. The house is completely dark except for a single spotlight that is focused on me. I am teaching an important lesson and the audience is completely enraptured, attending to my every word. Follow your dreams.

What do you get excited about?
What do you get excited about? Are there injustices in the world that particularly offend you? Does a particular sport or place thrill you? Do you love the ocean or the mountains? If you love scuba diving, you might enjoy working in a dive shop in Key West, Florida.

What are your particular talents?
What are your particular talents? Do you play the piano? Do you sing well? Do you play tennis well? Are you a good teacher? Are you a good salesperson? We all enjoy doing those things at which we excel. Follow your talents to your personal mission in life.

Logotherapy

Logotherapy is the name given to Victor Frankl's psychological theory. In *Man's Search for Meaning* Frankl describes his experience in the concentration camps of Nazi Germany. Frankl suggests that if people are able to find meaning in their personal tragedy, then they can live more easily with that tragedy.

A child who suffered a debilitating illness in his youth may discover that his personal mission in life is to relieve the suffering of children as a medical doctor. A woman who was raped may find meaning working for a rape crisis service. A survivor of a cult experience may take pride in the courage he discovered within himself to overcome its influence and use that pride to achieve his personal destiny. A victim of the communists in Russia might find the strength, courage, and vision from that experience to write a novel smashing for all time the malignant morality upon which communism is based.

Hopefully, you have lived a benign, untraumatic life. If not, perhaps you can find your life's work in your suffering.

Professional help

If none of these suggestions work, try career counseling. There are batteries of tests that can determine your interests and abilities. There are seminars and workshops that will guide you in choosing a career that you will love.

Remember there is nothing more important for an adult than discovering his or her personal destiny.

FULFILLING YOUR PERSONAL DESTINY IS THE MEANING OF YOUR LIFE

Most of us spend at least 45 hours per week, 40% of our waking lives, working and commuting to work. Your work should be the actual fulfillment of your personal mission, or it should take you in the direction of the fulfillment of your personal mission.

The Definitive Statement of the Purpose of My Life

Each of us should have a definitive statement of the purpose of our lives. This statement will guide us in our daily lives. It will be the standard by which we judge our daily actions. "Will this particular action take me toward my life's goal or away from it?"

You can have more than one purpose in your life if they do not conflict, for example, work and children.

The following are examples of a definitive statement of the purpose of a person's life.

- The purpose of my life is to create the Fellowship of Reason and to establish FOR as an important international institution in which rational individualists can celebrate their lives, enjoy art and fellowship, learn, reflect and meditate, and reorient themselves to their own self-chosen hierarchy of values and meaning.

- The purpose of my life is to raise three happy, healthy children to become rational, responsible, benevolent adults.

- The purpose of my life is to work for UPS, to learn everything about the company's operation, and to prepare myself to be the CEO of the company.

- The purpose of my life is to be a writer and to present in fiction the ideal man.

- The purpose of my life is to be the best software salesman at Computers-R-Us and to become a millionaire by saving and investing well by age 45. Then I will travel the world and see exotic places.

- The purpose of my life is to become a medical doctor, to go into family practice in a small town, and to deliver 1,000 babies.

FELLOWSHIP OF REASON

- The purpose of my life is to become a lawyer and then go into politics to defend freedom and advocate limited government.

- The purpose of my life is to become a research scientist and discover the cure for AIDS.

- The purpose of my life is to be the best garbage man I can be and to support my wife and children to the best of my ability.

- The purpose of my life is to compose beautiful music to complement Celebration at the Fellowship of Reason.

What is your definitive statement of the purpose of your life? Compose it now.

We encourage and actively assist the members of the Fellowship of Reason to make a definitive statement of the purpose of their lives. We use that statement in the "Look-Up Ritual" described in chapter 10. Our members use their own personal mission statements to make important choices every day of their lives.

Pitfalls to avoid

Unfortunately, it is very easy to get off one's own proper path. The reason is that other people and society want to *use* you for their own ends and they do not care whether you experience the rapture of being alive or not.

As a child you were probably taught to comply and conform. You were taught to deny your own interests for the sake of others. You were taught to delay gratification for a later reward. These socializing rules are not without merit in the context of childhood, but it takes true wisdom to apply them to a whole human life. When you became an adult, you became master of your own destiny. You are autonomous, self-responsible, and self-fulfilling. You need an explicit philosophy and a self-defined hierarchy of values to live. You need a morality.

There are many pitfalls on the way to the rest of your life. Their names are your parents, your peer group, the media, your teachers, your spouse, your children, and society—in short, other people's expectations. All of these people have an opinion about *your* own proper destiny and most of us are overly sensitive to their opinions. We should not be.

Parents

Young people need to be encouraged to do those things that they enjoy. Parents need to be particularly cautious about imposing their own dreams (realized or not) upon their children. Parents must avoid stealing the lives and happiness of their children by guiding them down the wrong paths to satisfy the parents' own unfulfilled desires.

Everyone has unique talents and tastes. A good parent will be attuned to her child's special skills and interests and encourage the child in those areas. It is often quite obvious both to parents and to the child where the young person's path lies.

Fictional accounts of parents ruining their children by directing them down wrong paths are legion. Peter Keating of Ayn Rand's *The Fountainhead* (1943) wanted to become a painter in his youth. Keating's mother nagged him to become an architect. He became a world-famous architect, but in the end he was miserably unhappy, having forsaken his destiny. His mother, too, suffered because she realized in the end that she contributed to her son's destruction.

As an adult, ignore your parents' preferences for your own personal career selection. Your parents' preferences are irrelevant.

For young adults, this is very difficult, since it involves changing a mode of behavior with which they have always lived. A young adult must change from the mode of obeying his parents to the mode of obeying himself.

Your peer group and "low" jobs

There are as many "high and noble goals" as there are people on this earth. I emphasize that your "high and noble goals" are high and noble by your own standards, not by mine or someone else's. Other people's opinions *do not count* in your determination of your own life goals.

For example, if you like working with boats and you want to be a dockhand at a marina, do it. Be the best dockhand you can be. Improve yourself in your job every day. Love your work. Revel in your career.

If your abilities are suited to moving trash and you like working out of doors with your hands, be a garbage man. Be the best garbage man you can be. You may find as you learn your job that you can make improvements in the business of moving garbage. You might move up in your company. You might someday own it. Or not.

I mention garbage collecting to emphasize that there are no bad or lowly jobs. There are, unfortunately, lazy, incompetent workers. Such workers have chosen to have lives that are defined by their own lazy and incompetent actions. Such people live meaningless, worthless (to themselves) lives. Such people are of little or no value as trading partners.

By the way, even a garbage man who does not advance to become the CEO of his company can become a millionaire over the course of his working life and retire in luxury. By saving $100 per week for thirty-five years at 9% interest, the garbage man will save a million dollars. Upon these same assumptions, he will have saved over 10 million dollars in his sixty-year working life.

Many people have skills beyond those necessary to be a garbage man. Such people will choose other occupations suitable to their talents and tastes.

One chief executive officer of United Parcel Service was once a delivery driver for the company. On the other hand, you might not be capable of achieving so much. Without a doubt you can do what you can do as best as you know how.

Everyone should choose a job or career in which she can revel. The reason a person should choose a career that she loves is so that she can be happy in her lifetime.

The media and the "proper" lifestyle

A recent correspondent to the editors of the Wall Street Journal complained that she could not pay for her car, her apartment, and daycare on the current minimum wage. She said she was not claiming that society owed her a living, just a decent wage. One respondent to that letter reported success at living on the minimum wage by sharing a modest loft with a roommate, taking the bus, enjoying walks in the city parks with his girlfriend, and eating lentils, potatoes, and other nutritious, but inexpensive foods. The first letter writer had been sold on the media-created myth that everyone should have a car and all manner of consumer goods. Her lifestyle *demanded* a certain income, which, in the absence of government force, she was unable to earn.

Most people are not so brazenly immoral as to demand that the government subsidize their profligate (in relation to their incomes) lifestyles. Rather, most people (including me in the past) spend beyond their means, borrow from credit cards, and work long hours at unpleasant, stress-filled jobs to pay for their prodigal lifestyles. Work is a necessary evil for such people. *Lifestyle* drives their career choice. They find no joy in their jobs. They live for the weekend or live to shop or live to travel or live to spend extravagantly.

Working to support prodigality is a mistake. It is the quintessential American mistake. Advertising encourages this mistake. Those people who allow their life goals to be dictated by television see success as the immediate possession of material goods—fancy cars, beautiful clothes, exotic vacations, an expensive house, all manner of consumer goods. These goods are the life goals of many people. Work is the means to their ends—consumer goods. It is not relevant to advertisers that their customers' work is unsatisfying or even positively unpleasant. The advertisers just want your money. That you become a dipsomaniac working at a meaningless job is of interest only to vendors of alcoholic beverages (your consumption helps their bottom line) and counseling services who hope to receive payment from your insurance company for treating you.

Please note that it is perfectly moral to want nice things. It is, however, unreasonable to expect that the ownership of a BMW automobile, for example, will give your life meaning. Furthermore, you may anticipate your fair share of stress and unhappiness if you borrow money, take an unpleasant job, and work long hours to the detriment of your family to acquire consumer goods.

The demands of an extravagant, beyond-your-means lifestyle cause stress. The stress must be managed in often-unhealthy ways, such as watching 21 hours of television per week, or excessive drinking or drug abuse, or spousal abuse or child abuse. Lifestyle should not drive work obligations or career choice.

The proper order of things is that your personal mission comes first. Follow your bliss and do what you love. From pursuit of your personal mission you will have a certain income. If your personal mission does not produce income, you will need to provide for your survival by some other means. After survival needs are met, your income should be directed toward the long-range goals of retirement and health care. From what remains after survival needs and savings, you should choose your lifestyle. If you can afford that BMW automobile, fine, if not, drive a less expensive car, take the bus, ride a bicycle, or walk.

Happiness comes not from working so you can spend, but from doing that which you *love* doing. The first and most important decision a person should make is not what type of car she would like to drive, but what will she *love* to do for the rest of her life.

A job as a means to your ends

Sometimes your personal mission cannot produce income immediately. You may have to work at some less-than-ideal job to support yourself modestly while pursuing your career. Such is the case for most graduate students. The law student who works as a waiter in a restaurant to pay his way through school is obviously not working in his chosen field. But he is on his way.

If your beloved activity is painting landscapes, make everything else subservient to painting landscapes. If your paintings are not selling yet, forget the BMW automobile. Since you must work for a living, choose a job as friendly as possible to your life's work. If you need to paint in the daytime for the light, have a night job to supply your survival needs. If you like to paint mountain views, get a job in Colorado with a mountain view. Get a job in a field that allows you to do work compatible with your talents and tastes. Do graphic design in Denver or paint murals for an outdoor advertising company.

Your career needs to take precedence over all of your other activities and values. It is critically important to your happiness that you spend the bulk of your lifetime, the 45 hours per week of career and commuting time, doing what you love.

Changing Personal Missions

We all make mistakes. Fortunately, given 60 years of working life, from age 22 to age 82 (let us be optimistic), we are not limited to only one personal mission. It may be that you will find after 20 years as a lawyer that you have accomplished all you wish in the field. You can change careers and start the Fellowship of Reason.

Some careers can be accomplished in less than a lifetime. The raising of children is precisely this type of occupation. Although the raising of children is the most important full time job in the world, it only takes 20 years per child. After the children are grown, the primary care-giver will need a new full time personal mission. In order to avoid a shocking void when the last child leaves the nest, you had better anticipate your obligation to set new "high and noble goals" for yourself.

Use Gradualism

When embarking upon the accomplishment of your lifetime goals, use gradualism. Gradualism means to break up the task into many small parts. Work on small, doable parts every day. You should work on your long-range goals at least one hour every day. This will be easy, since a major part of any "high and noble goal" will be the task of self-education about the goal. There is always time to read about and study your subject. You will need to become *the* expert in your field. Your "high and noble goal" is a lifetime task. Do not be surprised that it will take decades to accomplish. Self-help books on success advise that all great achievement is 1% inspiration and 99% perspiration, meaning that persistence pays off. The woman with the vision for her own future will succeed. If you do not know where you are going, you are unlikely to get there.

A World Full of People Following Their Bliss

As a side issue, consider the social benefits of a society in which everyone is on a personal mission. Whenever you come in contact with a trading partner, be it the clerk in the grocery store or your personal physician, that person would be having the time of her life in her job. She would be happy. She would be friendly. She would be superbly competent. What tremendous value we would receive from such trading partners. Such a world is to be sought after. Such a world will be achieved if the advice of this chapter is taken seriously.

Wholeness, Harmony, Radiance

Everyone has a hierarchy of values. At the top of your personal, self-chosen hierarchy is your definitive statement of the purpose of your life that you have just learned how to create. The other elements of your hierarchy of values are expressed in your revised life "time" inventory described in chapter 3. This structure has been named by others a "life theme" and a "system of goals and means." Some people accept the goals provided by genetic instructions (money, power, and sex). Some people accept the goals provided by the rules of society (work hard, watch TV, and buy consumer goods). A fortunate few understand the importance of choosing their own goals and means, their own personal mission in life. I have suggested that you follow your bliss, that you identify what it is that you love doing and make that your life's work.

Once you have defined your life theme, you must then implement it. You must constantly, I mean daily, check to see that you are on your path. Your life theme and system of goals and means must be *whole*, that is complete, including all necessary elements required for human happiness. Your actions must be in *harmony* with, consistent with, your life theme. When these two elements are present (wholeness and harmony), you can achieve *radiance*, happiness, flow, rapture, and bliss—different words for the same psychological event.

You now have the key to the meaning of life. Enjoy it, my friend.

Spirituality is the practice of being happy. A person is happy when he or she has a healthy soul. In the next chapter we will take a look at the human soul.

Chapter 5 — The Human Soul

> When you go to see some important personage, remember that there is an Other [universal reason] watching what happens from above, and that it is better to please this Other than that man. —Epictetus quoted in Hadot 1998, p. 121

> When I was a child, I talked like a child, I thought like a child, I reasoned like a child. When I became a man, I put childish ways behind me. —1 Corinthians 13:11

> [A]s man is a being of self-made wealth, so he is a being of self-made soul. —Rand 1957, p. 1020

> Indignation is the soul's defense against the wound of doubt about its own; it reorders the cosmos to support the justice of its cause. —Bloom 1987, p. 71

Members of the Fellowship of Reason have two things in common. First, our goal is happiness on earth. Second, our means is reason. Reason must be applied to the understanding of both existence and consciousness in order to achieve happiness. In this chapter we explore the nature of human consciousness.

Perhaps the greatest impediment to happiness is an individual's failure to question himself. Some people are *unwilling* to question themselves. To others the thought of questioning themselves does not even occur. Yet the truth is that in America in the twenty-first century external conditions are ideal for the achievement of personal happiness. The *only* barriers to happiness are within the individual's own soul. In order to achieve happiness, we must look within ourselves.

Common barriers to self-examination are hubris, anger, and fear. We must put aside these roadblocks before we can examine human consciousness.

Hubris

"Pride is the recognition of the fact that you are your own highest value and, like all of man's values, it has to be earned (Rand 1957, p. 1020)." *Pride has to be earned.*

When a child becomes an adolescent, he discovers that he is a unique individual, separate from his parents. He is astonished. He realizes that only he can speak for himself. As he learns of his own infinite potentialities he imagines himself realizing them. As the adolescent dashes through various potential lifetimes in his imagination in search of his own highest and best destiny, he may insolently announce his contempt for the discarded paths. The lives of his parents are very likely candidates for insolent dismissal. The great men and women of history may not escape his arrogance.

Sometimes an adolescent discovers our philosophy of reason and brings his adolescent insolence into the society of rational individualists. Our adolescent acolyte has, of course, accomplished nothing in his life. Yet he finds validation for his unearned pride in our philosophy of reason's declaration that pride is a virtue. When such an individual reaches adulthood he can be blocked by his inappropriate, adolescent hubris from healthy growth.

Ideas survive only if there is some truth in them. Although the idea that pride is a sin is false, it is true that if a person is unwilling to consider the possibility that he has not yet achieved moral perfection, he is unlikely to attempt personal moral progress. Pride is a virtue, but hubris—unearned and inappropriate pride—is a personal moral problem.

If we are to experience personal growth, unearned and inappropriate pride must be set aside.

Anger

The emotion of anger sometimes indicates that one's self-esteem has been attacked. A healthy self-esteem, though, cannot be undermined by others. A healthy self-esteem is based upon true facts about oneself, not upon the opinions or actions of others. Therefore, if one experiences anger at a non-physical personal attack, consider the possibility of a personal shortcoming.

One of my personal problems is that I have an abhorrence of conflict. The reason for my abhorrence of conflict is that I practiced law for twenty years and made a profession of handling the negotiations and lawsuits of others. As a result of dealing with conflict in over four thousand law cases, I became inappropriately averse to conflict in my personal life.

There is, or should be, give and take in every relationship. Human relations are a continuous negotiation. Conflict in relationships is necessary and appropriate.

I have been friends with a couple for many years. Both of them have very strong personalities. Over the course of our relationship, whenever a difference of opinion would come up, I would give in to their whims without a whimper. For example, while listening to my favorite country music station in the car, they said they hated country music. So, in order to avoid conflict, I changed the station. When choosing a restaurant, their preference was always where we ate together. Many examples of similar small sacrifices over the years of our relationship might be cited. One day I received a letter from one of them requesting that I do something that I thought dishonest—like (but not) duplicating a copyrighted video. I was furious. Lawyers do not do that kind of thing! My friend had finally presented me with a conflict that I could not avoid. I wrote a harsh letter rebuking my friend and cited all of the little offenses I could think of over the years.

My reaction was over blown. A normal person may have felt a mild righteous indignation and frankly refused to copy the tape. But fury?

I realized sometime later that I was angry for all the little sacrifices I had made to my personal "god-of-no-conflict." But all of those little sacrifices were my fault alone, not my friends'.

My friends, though wrong to ask me to do something dishonest, were treated unfairly by me. I was fully responsible for not standing up for my values with them over the years. I should not have inflicted my fury upon them for my many failures to stand up for myself. So I apologized to my friends and we resumed our friendship, though with perceptibly less enthusiasm.

I vowed never to commit such an error again. Unfortunately, a few years later, I found myself furious at another friend. Happily, before I let him have it, I realized I was making the same mistake again. Now, as a part of my spiritual exercises (see chapter 6), I include as one of my long-term concerns a reminder that I abhor conflict in the hope that I will not avoid engaging in appropriate negotiations with friends for my values.

Anger was a signal to me, not that my friend had offended, but that I had a chronic personal problem.

Anger is also a common response to criticism by another (or self-criticism). Should a friend suggest that I lose a few pounds, I might respond angrily that she too might lay off the French fries. How very inappropriate! I should be always on the lookout for ways to improve myself. Rather than responding to criticism by attacking a courageous and loving friend, I should instead ask myself if the criticism is true. And, if true, I should be thankful for my friend and proceed to address the problem.

Author and psychiatrist M. Scott Peck identifies a practice he calls "bracketing." Bracketing is the practice of withholding an angry response to criticism long enough to determine whether the criticism contains valuable information for personal growth.

If we are to obtain knowledge of our own souls, anger must be suspected as the possible sign of a personal problem.

FEAR

Fear is an individual's greatest block to self-knowledge. This rule applies to psychological truths, which we are examining here, as well as to physical truths. Everyone has heard a story about a person who had a suspicious mole, and, fearing the worst, avoided going to the doctor until it was too late. One of the axioms of our philosophy of reason is that existence precedes consciousness—what is *is* whether you choose to know it or not. Therefore, in the realm of both the body and the mind, it is best to know the true condition of your body and mind, in spite of your fear.

FELLOWSHIP OF REASON

Discovering One's Soul

Once you get past hubris, anger, and fear, it is possible to look within yourself and discover who you are. The human soul contains these parts: the other, the daemon, the emotions, reason, and your parents' child.

The other
Most people have a conscience. It is that little angel sitting on your right shoulder advising you to do right. Sometimes our conscience has learned false moral lessons and the angel sends us false data. But the fact is that it is there and it keeps on functioning according to its programming.

A more scientific take on this aspect of the human soul is that it is the faculty of the mind that identifies reality. Once the mind is exposed to the facts, the process of identification is, in some cases, automatic. The only way to avoid being presented with the results of the process is to actively repress the information. Repression can take the form of simply turning the mind's eye away, or physically acting out (being hyperactive or violent or angry or loud or hysterical) to distract oneself, or taking drugs or alcohol to dull one's awareness of the undesirable knowledge. Of course, the information remains in one's unconscious as an irritant.

Individuals who repress painful contents of the automatic identifying function of their minds make all the evil in the world possible.

Your daemon
Every adult has different experiences, interests, temperaments, intelligence, talents, learning, and physical capacities. Some have perfect 20/20 vision. Some have perfect hearing. Some have perfect pitch. Some are tall. Some are strong. Some are calm. Others are high strung. Some finished high school. Others are over thirty when they complete their specialized medical training. Some were victims of alcoholic parents. Others had tranquil, loving childhoods. Some play the piano. Others do not. Some are thoughtful in their manner of living. Others are impulsive.

Thousands of parameters, learned, genetic, and chosen combine to form the unique person that each of us is. Many of these parameters cannot be changed. Some of these parameters can be modified over time.

79

For example, an adult abused in childhood might enter psychotherapy and learn to effectively deal with his injuries. Another adult might learn to play the guitar. Another adult might decide to study philosophy and change his pattern of living from unconscious to conscious.

It is true, though, that by the time an adult starts reflecting about himself, he is largely a *fait accompli*—a thing done. That which is "done" or fixed or already in existence is the individual's "innate potential excellence," in the words of philosopher David L. Norton.

The ancient Greeks referred to the individual's innate potential excellence as his "daemon," or little god. One's daemon resides within the individual. According to the Greeks, it is the individual's job to learn who his daemon is and make real (actualize) that potential. The emotional state that accompanies the actualization of one's daemon is eudaemonia, in the Greek. Eudaemonia is often translated as "happiness." The roots of the word suggest that "well-being" is a better translation.

As an adult, the individual cannot whimsically choose just any career. I, for example, cannot choose to be a mother—no uterus. I cannot choose to be an NBA star. I am not tall enough, young enough, strong enough, or talented enough. On the other hand, there are things that I am well suited to be. For example, I enjoy staying home and looking after my son. I am lucky enough to have a working wife who enjoys her job and is happy allowing me to stay at home. I do not need the usual accoutrements of manhood (powerful job, expensive car, et cetera) to be content. I am happy and proud to be a "Mr. Mom."

The point is that the unique experiences, interests, temperaments, intelligence, talents, learning, and physical capacities of each adult, as a matter of fact, *have an optimal use*. Everyone is especially well suited for something. It is every individual's job to find out exactly what that optimal use of himself is. That optimal use of oneself is his daemon. This is the meaning of the Greek expression, "Know thyself."

Some people will rebel at the thought that their horizons are not limitless or that their optimal life paths are defined. But the assumption underlying that rebellion is the thought that one will not enjoy realizing his innate potential excellence—I will say his destiny. Not true. That which one does best is that which one enjoys doing most.

FELLOWSHIP OF REASON

Not only can I not be a mother, I have no desire to be one. Not only can I not be an NBA star, the thought holds zero interest for me. No one wants to fail. We all want to succeed. If each of us maximizes his potential, he will be successful in life and, simultaneously, happy. This is the meaning of the other expression from antiquity, "Become who you are."

The responsibility of knowing yourself and becoming who you are is dramatized in fiction very frequently. The dramatic choice is to live a conventional life (the life other people expect you to live) or to live an authentic life (your own true life). There are many examples: Peter Keating, a character in Ayn Rand's *The Fountainhead*, lived the conventional life of an architect (because of the expectations of his mother and various "others") and sacrificed his own true love—painting. The artist forced by his parents to become a businessman is a classic story, often told. The theme of the Academy Award–winning movie *American Beauty* is that an authentic life is preferable to the conventional life. The Disney animated classic *Mulan* shows a young girl breaking the bounds of convention at the risk of her own life.

Those who rebel against the idea that they have an innate potential destiny might consider whose life they are living now—one of their own choice or some pattern they have fallen into. My case is not unique. I practiced law for twenty years. In the first months of my practice I would feel ill while driving by my office on the weekends. I was not even going in. I was just driving by the building on the way to the store or whatever. By seeing the outside of the building, I was reminded of all the problems waiting for me Monday morning. In twenty years, it never got better. As a young adult I did not deliberately choose the law. My father was a lawyer. My grandfather was a lawyer. I am a fifth generation lawyer. I never thought of being anything else. I was not living my own choice, but my family history.

Know who you are. Become who you are.

Reason

Reason is the handmaiden of emotions. Human beings do not ultimately desire to be reasonable, but to have deep experiences of being alive—powerful, sacred emotions—the feelings one experiences when in love, when holding one's infant child, when performing one's sacred mission in life. As it happens, though, reason is the only means to life—health and happiness. Only happiness is an end in itself.

Since reason is man's means of survival, he had better use it. Reason operates when one turns his attention to a subject and attempts to discover the facts. Reason is a selective focus. One's capacity to reason is not dependent upon his intelligence. Every normal human being can and should (if he is to achieve health and happiness) reason. One should practice the habit of turning his attention to his inner condition as well as to his outer circumstances.

Emotions

Among the inner conditions to which one should attend are one's emotions. Here are some negative emotions: envy, gloating, jealousy, anger, rage, fear, disgust, aversion, dislike, hate, fear, greed, avarice, hubris, shame, embarrassment, sadness, frustration, remorse, guilt, anxiety, suffering, and worry. Here are some positive emotions: pride, efficacy, pleasure, contentment, satisfaction, joy, elation, ecstasy, gratitude, thankfulness, blissfulness, sacred being, reverence, worshipfulness, happiness, friendship, admiration, desire, sexual desire, excitement, love, generosity, charity, magnanimity, confidence, hope, anticipation, righteous indignation, and ambition.

All of these emotions are signals. The light of reason should be turned upon all of these emotions. The facts giving rise to them should be checked before action is taken. You should work to eliminate the negative emotions from your life. You should work to bring about circumstances that cause positive emotions in your life. In order to achieve a preponderance of positive emotions in your life, effort is required.

A simple example—an envious friend takes too many opportunities to call your attention to potential difficulties in your life. His purpose is not to help you avoid difficulty, but to take away your pleasure in your successes, because he envies those successes. Solution—find a new friend. Move away from or change circumstances productive of negative emotions. Move toward and create circumstances productive of positive emotions.

Your parents' child

Everyone is profoundly influenced by his parents. As I have said, I became a lawyer without really even thinking about it. Many people follow in their parents' footsteps by default. If your are is to live consciously, it is important to be aware that you may be becoming your parent.

There is, of course, nothing necessarily wrong with reliving your parent's life. They may have had perfectly good lives worthy of emulation. On the other hand, it is unlikely that you would have read this book to this point if you were satisfied imitating your parents.

Your parents have shaped a part of you. As an autonomous, self-knowledgeable, self-responsible, self-fulfilling adult seeking excellence, you would do well to evaluate just what type of people your parents were. Most people, including me, are blind to the fact that they have become their parent. This is true with positive or neutral features of the parent. It might also be true of very negative features of a parent. Tragically, some people emulate their abusive or neglectful parents. Rarely does a person have sufficient self-awareness to realize this without professional help.

Conclusion to discovering one's soul

A human being is not two separate things—mind and body. A human being is a unified being of body and mind. There are not literally five structures in a human consciousness—the other, the daemon, reason, the emotions, and the parent's child. These categories are tools for thinking about the unified whole that is the human mind. I assert that in order to be happy one must use reason to examine the world about him and his own spiritual nature. In the twenty-first century, circumstances are supremely auspicious for the achievement of material success. The only impediment to happiness for most people is within their own souls. That is where most of us must direct our attentions in our quest for spiritual bliss.

THE STAGES OF LIFE

An important piece of knowledge concerning the human soul is an understanding of the various stages of life through which an individual passes. Each stage of life has its own rules. Knowing those rules, when they apply, and when they become obsolete is crucial for successful living. Knowing about the early stages is important in our role as parents and in being able to identify childhood and adolescent behaviors in ourselves that are inappropriate as an adult.

According to philosopher David L. Norton, among others, there are four stages of the life of man—childhood, adolescence, maturity, and old age. With respect to each stage I will note the epiphany that begins each stage, the essential problem of the stage, who bears the responsibility for you, the primary virtues of the stage, and an example of the fallacy of anachronism applicable to each stage. The fallacy of anachronism is the imposition upon one stage of human life an expectation applicable to a different stage.

Childhood

Like all stages of human life, childhood begins with an epiphany—the epiphany of birth. No one can remember what it was like to be squeezed from the peaceful, dark, muffled, warm, fluid, weightless place within his mother's womb into the dangerous, bright, noisy, cold, air-filled, gravity-rules world in which we all live. I imagine, though, that it was shocking. Each stage of life begins with a shocking discovery.

The essential problem of childhood is the child's complete and utter dependency. A child, though, is not a problem to herself. A child is a problem for her parents. She cannot survive without external assistance. All of the child's primary needs must come from her parents. Among the needs are food, shelter, clothing, and love. The love of others in childhood is an important basis for self-love later in life.

Although a child has inborn qualities and will ultimately acquire volition, much of what the child is to become is determined by the child's parents. For example, if the child is not to become an adult who will need to spend the rest of her life in therapy or prison, her parents will need to love her rather than hate her.

When a couple decide to have a child, part of their decision-making process needs to be a consideration of what type of adult human being they wish to create. The creation of a child who will enter adulthood with a healthy soul is made possible by a twenty-year commitment to good parenting by the couple. The creation of a child who will enter adulthood with a damaged or sick soul is caused by another type of couple. Bad parenting is the root of all evil.

The primary virtue of childhood is the child's receptivity to the input of his parents and his environment.

An example of the fallacy of anachronism as applied to childhood is an inappropriate "respect" for the child's "authority." Children are born utterly helpless. As they grow the degree of their helplessness slowly decreases. A sensitive parent will not delegate authority to a child prematurely and inappropriately. For example, a wise parent will not allow his child to choose the food she eats. Rather, the wise parent serves balanced, healthy foods to his child. Furthermore, a wise parent does not allow his child to determine an appropriate bedtime, but rather prescribes the proper time for the child. A child simply does not have the information necessary to make most of the many choices that must be made. Most of the choices affecting the life of a child are appropriately made finally and authoritatively by the child's parents.

Children are entitled to live their lives subject to an unquestionable and loving authority. A child should not be presented with unsolved problems. An unsolved problem demands a solution. Presenting a child with a problem the child knows he is completely incapable and unprepared to resolve is a great injustice.

Adolescence

Adolescence begins when the individual discovers that she is a unique individual separate from her parents. The epiphany that begins adolescence is the self-awareness of one's capacity for volition. The adolescent suddenly realizes that she is autonomous. She realizes that her "I" is something only she can ever know and for whom only she can speak.

An essential task of adolescence is the tender care and encouragement of her inner voice, her own autonomy. The adolescent must render her inner voice authoritative and trustworthy. The adolescent is acquiring knowledge that will allow her in adulthood to attain autonomy, self-knowledge, self-responsibility, self-fulfillment, and excellence.

An adolescent is a problem for herself and for her parents.

The adolescent's job is to gain knowledge about the world upon which to base the choices she will make as an adult. The adolescent must explore life's ultimate possibilities without making any final commitments. She must avoid final commitments because she does not yet have enough information upon which to base them. Some examples of final commitments to be avoided in adolescence are parenthood and marriage.

Among the choices to be explored in adolescence are different personality types for friends and spouses, various sources of pleasure, various sources of self-worth, marriage or bachelorhood, children or not, and various careers. The adolescent must mentally explore different possible lifestyles in order that she can choose among them as an adult.

Two important virtues of adolescence are enthusiasm and courage. Courage comes naturally to adolescents given their unawareness of their own mortality. Enthusiasm is necessary for the exploration of her potentialities.

The job of an adolescent is to explore the various choices that she must ultimately make as an adult. Therefore, necessarily an adolescent will be seen to be moving from one enthusiasm to another, from one boyfriend to another, from one career interest to another. This is as it should be.

The fallacy of anachronism is committed with respect to adolescence when an adult encourages the adolescent to pick one thing and stick with it. While for adults final choices are necessary and appropriate, adolescence is the only opportunity for uncommitted experimentation with the many possibilities life has to offer.

Adulthood

And now we come to the epiphany that marks the transition from adolescence to maturity—"Someday, I must die." Adulthood begins when the individual realizes that his lifetime is finite.

The adult is no longer a problem for his parents. The adult is uniquely his own problem. Parents of adult children who are unwilling to let their adult children go and adults who want to remain children sometimes fail to recognize this fact, thereby committing the fallacy of anachronism.

The realization that one's life is finite carries with it the corollary knowledge that only a limited amount of time remains in which one can do all that one desires.

FELLOWSHIP OF REASON

What shall I do? Who shall I become? Adolescent exploration has provided the individual with some data upon which to make a decision. Even so, final decisions need not yet be made.

Many young adults are still searching for their life's work. In my experience the person who knows from age 9 that she wants to be a writer, or from age 12 that he wants to be a psychologist, or from age 7 that she wants to be a nurse is rare. Most of us do not know in young adulthood what our personal mission in life is to be.

In the words of Joseph Campbell, the young adult should look in the direction of his bliss, not his parents' bliss, not his friends' bliss, not society's bliss, but his own bliss.

The problem of finding your life's work is the great problem of adulthood. I call this problem the problem of meaning. The other problem of adulthood is the problem of survival. An autonomous, self-knowledgeable, self-responsible, self-fulfilling, and excellent adult must earn a living.

The demands of earning a living are often experienced as in conflict with the pursuit of your personal mission—that one thing only you can do. But it need not be if you earn a living in the direction of your bliss.

An adolescent explores life's possibilities largely in her imagination. A young adult can make those adolescent thought experiments concrete. As indicated earlier, that one thing only you can do, your personal destiny, may not yet be known to you. In order to find your bliss you can accumulate real-life experience as data for your search.

The virtues of adulthood are all of those virtues that our philosophy recognizes, including reason, purpose, and self-esteem.

I said that a child is entitled to an unquestionable and loving authority. When the need for and entitlement to an unquestionable authority is carried forward into adulthood the fallacy of anachronism is committed. An unquestionable authority in adulthood interferes with adult autonomy, self-knowledge, self-responsibility, self-fulfillment, and excellence. It is this particular fallacy that results in the desperate need for a god among some adults. An adult who needs a god is an adult who has failed to give up the childhood need for and entitlement to an unquestionable and loving authority. In the language of mythology (see chapter 11), an adult who needs God is a person who has refused the call to adventure of psychological maturity.

87

Another example of the fallacy of anachronism in adulthood is bringing forward from adolescence the desire to experiment with life's possibilities without commitment. The desire to change spouses like one might change dating partners is a concrete instance.

Old age/Decrepitude

Old age begins with the recognition the one no longer has any future.

In old age, one is no longer a problem to his parents. They are long dead. More importantly, one is no longer a problem even to himself. He is a *fait accompli*, a thing done. He has finished his life's work. He has completed his life's plan.

The primary virtue of old age is gratitude—gratitude for the beautiful life one has lived. As Joseph Campbell said in the last year of his life, "No matter what seat you have at the opera, it's always a great show."

The fallacy of anachronism is manifested at this stage of life by the experience of anger or fear that one no longer has a future. One should have been preparing for this day from the moment of the epiphany of adulthood—"Someday, I must die."

In the fullness of time, I will come to know that I, in truth, have no future. Perhaps a terminal illness will afflict me. Perhaps an infirmity will make further strivings impossible. Then, with my life complete, I will look back on the whole of my existence and I will see, in panoramic view, me. I hope that I will know that my life was good, that it was beautiful, that it was true. I will draw the comforter up to my chin against the chill of the thrill I feel from the view on this my peak at the end of time. "O my soul, bless you for you are whole. I have lived!"

Conclusion to stages of life

As an adult, if you act in accordance with your deepest personal inclinations, all of your actions will be motivated by love—love for the realization of your own innate potential excellence. You will be enthusiastic, driven, and excellent.

Some alternatives to motivation by love are motivation by need, desire, vanity, guilt, shame, or some extrinsically imposed duty.

A life lived for the love of your own innate potential excellence concludes with the knowledge: "I lived the life which was my own." "My life was necessary." "My life had meaning." "I would not exchange places with any other." Such a person envies no one.

Those are the internal rewards for fulfilling your destiny. They are sufficient.

But notice that the world too gets a reward when individuals pursue their own innate potential excellence. A job that needs doing—your job—is being done by the best possible person in the world for the job and it is being done with excellence. You, the doer of the job, are happy, benevolent, and generous.

It is ironic that many people wish for immortality and yet waste the few precious years that they are given. The knowledge that "Someday, I must die" is the ultimate call to adventure. It is the statement that there is no time to lose. Get about living your life now. Make every day count. Fill every day with meaning. You will know you are succeeding if you go to bed at night with the thought "Today, I have lived my life well."

IMMORTALITY

The human soul is not immortal. If it were, we would have all the time in the world (eternity) to get it (the soul) right. We should all seek to have a healthy soul. Since our time is limited, the health of one's soul is an urgent matter requiring immediate and daily attention. The Fellowship of Reason nurtures healthy souls.

In the next chapter, we will learn how to improve our souls. We shall also reveal the natural, non-mystical referents of the HolyTrinity—God the Father, God the Son, and God the Holy Spirit.

Chapter 6—Spiritual Exercise

Spirituality is the practice of being happy.   —Anonymous

[Spiritual exercise or the philosophic act] raises the individual from an inauthentic condition of life, darkened by unconsciousness and harassed by worry, to an authentic state of life, in which he attains self-consciousness, an exact vision of the world, inner peace, and freedom.   —Hadot 1995, p. 83

[H]ow is it possible to practice spiritual exercises in the twentieth century?. . . There can be no question, of course, of mechanically imitating stereotyped schemas. After all, did not Socrates and Plato urge their disciples to find the solutions they needed by themselves?   —Hadot 1995, p. 108

She was looking up at the face of a man who knelt by her side, and she knew that in all the years behind her, *this* is what she would have given her life to see: a face that bore no mark of pain or fear or guilt.   —Rand 1957, p. 701

In order for a religion to flourish it must help people with important needs. Christianity flourished in antiquity because it helped people with an important need. Christianity enabled people to achieve happiness.

The ability to help people achieve happiness was not, however, unique to Christianity. The philosophical practices of the ancient Greeks and Romans enabled practitioners to achieve happiness. Pierre Hadot makes this important point in his book *Philosophy as a Way of Life* .

According to Hadot, the philosophic act or spiritual practice had the goal of achieving a certain mental state in the mind of the practitioner. Specifically, the goal was to bring peace to a worried mind. The worries of the mind can be categorized by the time period to which the worry relates—the past, the present, or the future.

Worries about the past can be classified as guilt (harm to another caused by your own moral wrong), shame (harm to yourself caused by your own moral wrong), hate (harm to yourself or another caused by the moral wrong of another), or regret (harm to yourself or another not caused by a moral wrong).

Worries about the future can be classified as cowardice, fear of death, fear of injustice, and fear of bad outcomes.

Worries about the present can be classified as anger, jealousy, or suffering pertaining to presently inflicted pain or illness. Other categories exist.

All of these worries can be repressed, experienced without resolution, or resolved. Many philosophic schools of antiquity had spiritual practices designed to resolve these categories of worries rather than actively repressing them or passively experiencing them without resolution.

Our mental state consists of more than just worries. There are, happily, mental pleasures. Relating to the past one can experience gratitude, pride, and fond memory. Relating to the future one can experience hope, courage, and excitement. Relating to the present one can experience love, joy, and desire. Other categories exist.

The ideal state of being is one *without* all the worries (guilt, shame, hate, regret, cowardice, fear, anger, jealousy, and suffering) and *with* all the mental pleasures (gratitude, pride, fond memory, hope, courage, excitement, love, joy, and desire).

Saul of Tarsus (10?–67?), who became the Apostle Paul, was the author of thirteen books of the New Testament. As the founder of many churches he was an important figure in the rise of Christianity. Since he was born in Turkey, traveled in Greece, and died in Rome, he was certainly acquainted with the philosophic schools of his time. Paul knew about spiritual exercise.

As the reader will shortly discover, spiritual exercise *as a philosophic act* requires significant mental effort. Spiritual exercise as practiced by the ancient philosophic schools was not easy. For Christians, though, Paul removed the work from spiritual exercise.

According to Christian doctrine, God the Father awards eternal life and divine justice to the faithful. A believer is thus relieved of the fear of death and injustice in the future. According to Christian doctrine, Jesus Christ died to save us from our sins. A believer is thus relieved of the pain of guilt for past transgressions. According to Christian doctrine, the Holy Spirit is the concrete reward of joy in the present. A believer is thus granted happiness in the present. The price of eternal life, justice, forgiveness, and happiness is, for Christians, faith.

The worries of mankind are divided, as I have said, into three temporal categories—past, present, and future. The Holy Trinity of Christianity relates to these three temporal categories. God the Father pertains to the future. Jesus Christ pertains to the past. The Holy Spirit pertains to the present.

Paul invented a doctrine that achieved the results of spiritual exercise without the mental work required by the spiritual exercises of the philosophic schools of antiquity. "For it is by grace you have been saved, through faith—and this not from yourselves, it is the gift of God—not by works, so that no one can boast (Ephesians 2:8–9)." But compare James 2:26, "As the body without the spirit is dead, so faith without deeds is dead." The question of faith versus works has been a hot theological topic since the Reformation.

The change in the rate of adoption of a particular spiritual practice might be expected to increase if the requirement of mental effort or *work* associated with the spiritual practice was eliminated or reduced. This is a simple economic principle—when price goes down, demand goes up. Christianity removed all the mental work from spiritual exercise. Christianity is "bargain basement" spiritual practice. It sold well in antiquity. It continues to sell today.

The achievement of happiness through faith is an important reason for the success of Christianity.

If Christianity results in happiness, why not become a Christian? Happiness is, after all, what we are all after. The reason is that Christian faith (either alone or with altruistic works) does not actually solve real-life problems. Wrongs remain unrighted. Justice and good outcomes require human effort. And eternal life is wishful thinking. The happiness achieved is based upon self-deception reinforced by the cult.

Members of the Fellowship of Reason insist on real solutions. Suggested real solutions follow.

EXAMINATION OF CONSCIENCE (PAST)

The reason people do philosophy or religion or television or drugs is this—they want to be happy or at least not in pain. Happiness does not happen by chance, and drugs and television will certainly not bring it to you. It is an individual human being's achievement. To arrive at happiness, an emotional state, you must deal with emotions pertaining to three periods of time—your feelings about the past, your feelings about your present circumstances, and your feelings about the future. Many people take whatever their feelings are about their past, present, and future as givens and not subject to change. Some people even take obstinate pride in their foolish feelings on the unstated premise that "if it's me, it must be right." But emotions *are* subject to change. The process is fourfold: First, you must identify the facts, both existential and spiritual (the worldly circumstances and your mental contents) that give rise to the emotion you would like to change. Second, you should consider whether your understanding of the facts or your perspective on the facts is correct and complete. Third, you must determine what, if any, action is possible with respect to the existing facts. If appropriate action is possible, it must be taken. Fourth, you must accept responsibility for the facts and fully experience the related emotion. Let us take each of these steps in turn.

One of the first jobs of my youth ended badly. My probationary period of employment ended and I was told I would not be hired. I was angry. As I left my employer's office for the last time I took some office supplies with me, a few pens and a pad of paper. I stole from my employer. Some weeks later I returned the items with a cover story I have forgotten.

I am ashamed of myself. I received no significant benefit from the theft. I certainly did not feel better as a result. I felt bad, guilty. I did not succeed in getting "even," assuming that is what I had in mind. I merely diminished myself in my own eyes.

Even now this theft is a source of pain. How am I to deal with it?

Following my suggestion that there are four steps to modifying unhappy emotions, I notice that by stating the problem I have identified most of the pertinent objective facts. Other facts that may be useful include the fact that the incident occurred over twenty-five years ago and the employer corporation no longer exists. An important subjective fact is that the source of my shame is my evaluation of my act as morally wrong. In my judgment people should deal with one another voluntarily. Obviously, there will be times when one party wants a relationship and the other party does not. In this circumstance there will be no relationship and one party will be disappointed. That is life.

Next I shall consider whether my understanding of or perspective on the facts is correct.

The reader may be irritated by the smallness of the example and think me odd for recalling such a trivial event. I confess to being odd. It is very important to me to be right. Deep down everyone is like this. I remember a scene in a movie in which the heroine, facing imminent death in a worldwide cataclysm, seeks to reconcile with her father. Her first act of reconciliation is to confess to having stolen a small amount of money from his wallet when she was a child. The father in turn confesses that he accidentally dropped her on her head when she was a child. This emotionally powerful scene suggests to me the idea that confession is good for the soul. More concretely, confession allows a person to let go of feelings of guilt concerning some action he personally considers bad.

The movie scene also suggests to me another important factor in evaluating my own sin. Age and experience matter in evaluating human action. A sin committed in youth may not be as heinous as the same sin committed later in life.

As applied to my own circumstance, I observe that while I was legally an adult and should have behaved better, I was still in school and having my first employment experience. I was still learning. I learned a very important lesson from my bad act—a lifetime of grief can follow the commission of actions that you yourself regard as immoral. My victim was not hurt and so my grief need not disable me.

Next I must consider whether I can take any action. Fortunately for me

I did make restitution. I did not, however, confess and apologize. The prospect of confessing is not pleasant. Could I stand the humiliation? Is it worth it given that the act happened over twenty-five years ago? Who would benefit? I sense that I would benefit from confessing. If my employer responded to my confession with a knowing chuckle and laughingly said, "You are forgiven, Martin," I could put the episode behind me. My guilt would be purged. Although my employer would not enjoy any monetary benefit, he might benefit morally by my example. A significant problem with this course of action for me is the fact that the employer was a corporation and no longer exists.

Finally, I reach the fourth step in dealing with guilt and that is to take responsibility for the action and learn to live with it. Sometimes no action is possible to relieve guilt and one's perspective of the facts is all too clear. In my case, the former employer is no more and an apology cannot be made. Also, although the actions were committed in my youth, I should have acted otherwise. I must, therefore, within my own soul take responsibility for my actions. I committed a theft. I know that theft is morally wrong. I do feel guilty. I presently experience that guilt. I do not repress it. My guilt will be a permanent part of my psyche. I must accept the fact. On the other hand, in the scheme of sins, mine is small and I have learned an important lesson. I will commit no more sins of this type.

I tell this story to illustrate the process by which one might clean up and clear out the debris of guilt in his mind. Guilt must be purged as much as possible in order to prepare your soul for happiness.

Obviously, it is much easier to avoid bad action than to find redemption.

EXPERIENCE OF REPRESSED PAIN (PAST)

I observed in the last section that guilt from the past can interfere with happiness in the present. In this section we will consider painful memories other than guilt.

Many years ago I went to Gatlinburg, Tennessee to ski. At the base of the mountain I saw a turning post designed to pull novice skiers around in a circle. I grabbed onto the device and was pulled around on my skis.

Suddenly an attendant started screaming at me. Apparently I was violating a rule. She abused me unmercifully. I was utterly humiliated and I slunk away. For years, whenever I heard mention of Gatlinburg, my mind actively repressed the memory of the incident. I realized, finally, that repression requires mental work, takes time, and blocks happiness. The next time I noticed my mind moving to repress the memory of my Gatlinburg humiliation I decided enough was enough. I determined to reach down into my memory of the event and fully explore and experience the humiliation I had so long avoided. I imagined myself back in Gatlinburg. I pictured the youthful attendant lashing me with her words. I felt my humiliation as deeply as I could. I tried to cry.

Since allowing myself to experience that humiliation more fully, I never again found myself repressing the memory of Gatlinburg. The memory is still unpleasant, but it is not so unpleasant that I block it out of my mind.

Everyone experiences humiliation, shame, embarrassment, abuse, and loss. Hopefully your own horrors are as banal as mine. In dealing with repressed painful memories, some people may need professional help because the pain is so great. I am reminded of Pat Conroy's powerful novel *The Prince of Tides*. The hero of this story, the hero's twin sister, and his mother are the victims of a home invasion and rape by convicts. The hero's older brother comes home and interrupts the attack. The convicts are killed. At the mother's insistence, she and the three young children bury the bodies of the convicts and conceal all evidence of the crimes from their father and the authorities. The two youngest children attempt to repress their own memories of these traumatic events. The terrible psychological toll on the children is the subject of the book.

The Prince of Tides ends happily with the twins, under the guidance of a psychiatrist, recalling the horrible events of their childhood, experiencing their pain, and moving beyond the pain to a happier life.

In order to achieve full happiness in the present, each of us must address the issue of repressed painful memories with or without professional help.

Look the Devil in the Face (Future)

It is well to remember our purpose. Our goal is happiness now. However, we find that our minds contain clutter and debris that interfere with happiness now. Through the examination of the clutter and debris in our minds, we hope to clean it up and clear it out of our minds. The activity of working on the contents of our mind to effect changes in our mental state is called spiritual exercise. Just like you engage in a fitness regimen including stomach crunches to rid your mid-section of fat-filled love handles, so you engage in various mental exercises, discussed in this chapter, in order to rid your mind of worrisome content.

The future is a constant source of anxiety for most people. Known problems and their possible outcomes loom. Potential problems pester the paranoid (like me) with active imaginations. Just as we have allowed guilt and pain to linger in our minds for years by passive avoidance or active repression, so are future fears often dealt with by passive avoidance or active repression. A sometimes-useful technique for dealing with fear of the future is to actually consider the worst possible outcome and how it might be handled.

I have a dear friend who is a lawyer. Many years ago he was a one-percent partner in a flashy law firm. The boss was the kind of man who loved extravagant displays of wealth. A person paying their own legal fees would turn around and walk out of my friend's big-city law office upon seeing the glittering lobby tiled in marble, complete with grand piano. The boss had an airplane, a yacht, and chauffeur-driven limousines. He was paying the highest rent in the big city. He had expensive offices in other cities. Now the magic of my friend's deal with the boss was that while my friend shared in only one percent of the profits and had little or no say in the conduct of the partnership, he was exposed by law to all the partnership liabilities. Well, the flashy law firm went bust. The law firm could not pay the rent in one of its other city offices. So the landlord sued all the partners. My friend was sued, not in his home state, but in a state five hundred miles away, for an office that was not his, simply because of his status as partner. My friend was a defendant in a two-million-dollar lawsuit.

Being a defendant in a multi-million-dollar lawsuit is bad enough. But, if you are a lawyer (and I am a lawyer), being sued is just about the worst thing you can imagine. My friend called me.

I flew to visit my friend to talk with him about the impending ruin of his career and family. I told him to go and talk with a bankruptcy lawyer. (Filing for bankruptcy is the second worst thing a lawyer can imagine.) I did not think he would really have to file for bankruptcy protection. I did, however, suggest that he must be prepared to take that step if the financial security of his wife and three children was seriously threatened.

I told him to hire a lawyer to deal with the two-million-dollar lawsuit.

The bankruptcy lawyer reported good news. Under the law of my friend's home state, his family home would not be at risk even in the event of a calamitous monetary judgment.

The result of looking at the worst possible outcome in my friend's case was an immediate reduction in anxiety. By hiring a competent professional to deal with the lawsuit he effectively delegated responsibility for the case. My friend was able to breathe again and to live with the years of litigation that followed.

We all have fears of the future that intrude upon our enjoyment of the present. Rather than avoiding thinking about the problem, try to imagine the worst possible outcome and how that worst of all possible outcomes might be handled. Then proceed to effectively deal with the future in the present. Once you have done these two things, one mental and one existential, put aside your fear of the future and enjoy your sacred present.

DEATH (FUTURE)

"I am completely fulfilled. I have lived a full life. I could die now content." I said that to myself outside of math class when I was eighteen. I do not remember the specific details giving rise to that blessed feeling, but I know the circumstances—my high-school girlfriend had recently let me know that she loved me, very likely in a deeply intimate way.

Today, though I feel very fulfilled, I am not ready to die, primarily because I have unfinished projects, not the least of which is the raising of my son to adulthood. In that parental sentiment is a clue to the fear of death.

The fear of death is actually the fear of leaving important experiences unlived. Tragically, many people fail to live authentically. They live the lives that others expect them to live, secretly hoping that one day, when their duty to others is fulfilled, they will live their own lives. A premature death for such a person means never to have lived his own life at all. Now there is a horror—not death, but never to have lived.

A spiritual exercise that works against a fear of death is the living of an authentic life. An authentic life is the fulfillment your own highest destiny as opposed to the life another expects you to live.

The knowledge that you are mortal is actually something that *should* be carried with you every day. Unlike guilt, repressed pain, or fear of an adverse outcome short of death, awareness of your mortality serves as a powerful guide and motivator to right action.

Daily Spiritual Exercise

With spiritual exercise, there are two secrets to success. The first secret is that the exercise must be objective. By that I mean it must be an event in the world as opposed to a purely mental event. There are two ways to make spiritual exercise a worldly event. One way is to engage in the exercise orally with at least one interlocutor. The other way is to write out the exercise in a personal journal or notebook. The second way has the virtues of convenience and privacy and will undoubtedly be the usual method. People in spiritual *crisis* will, on the other hand, wisely choose to engage in spiritual exercise orally by talking with a spouse, a friend, a counselor, a psychologist, or a psychiatrist. *Thinking alone is not sufficient as spiritual exercise.*

The second secret of success with spiritual exercise is that the exercise must be performed on a regular basis. Daily performance is optimal. Every other day is okay. If the exercise is performed less than every other day, it is not being experienced as valuable and will most likely be discontinued.

The daily spiritual exercise involves, in essence, thinking about your life and writing down those thoughts. The result of good thinking about your life should be right action and happiness.

The notebook

Begin by purchasing a spiral-bound or loose-leaf lined notebook. Lay the book flat and open so that two lined sheets of paper present themselves to the left and right of the spiral binding. On the left sheet of paper write, "What's good about my life now?"

Since the reason for performing spiritual exercise is to become happier, it is appropriate to begin the journey to happiness by taking a current inventory of what you already have to be happy about. This list should be extensive at first. You may want to include the wonderful fact of your existence, the beautiful weather you might be enjoying at the moment, the friends and loved ones that you enjoy, your favorite pastime, anything that exists that brings you pleasure and happiness is properly included on this list.

On the right sheet of paper write the sentence "What do I wish to do today?" This is nothing more than a common "to do" list. It does not take much time to enumerate that tasks that you would like to complete during the day. By considering them in advance you are able to order them in a meaningful and efficient way. Most important by planning your day and executing your plan, you insure that your day has a meaning you intend. The alternative is to dissipate the precious time of your life in an haphazard manner.

Turn the page to reveal two new blank sheets of paper. On the left page write the phrase "Long-term concerns." We all have long-term projects of body and soul, like improving our primary relationships, personal fitness, weight loss, saving for a major purchase, quitting smoking, whatever. In this section name your long-term concern or goal, state why you want to resolve the issue or achieve the goal, and detail how you specifically plan today to address that concern or make progress toward achieving that goal.

On the right sheet of paper write the phrase "Short-term concerns." On some days problems arise that are a source of anxiety. Rather than ignoring the problem, name the problem, write what interests of yours are threatened, and write what you can do today to influence a good outcome. If you cannot influence the outcome, write down why worrying about the problem to the detriment of your otherwise happy day will be of value. If worrying about the problem will not enhance your life and happiness, write down whether it is possible for you to leave the issue temporarily and not worry about it until action is necessary and appropriate.

Your morning spiritual exercises complete, you are ready to face the day.

At the end of the day write the sentence "How did I do today?" Summarize your success in completing your "to do" list and dealing with your long and short-term concerns.

And finally just before going to sleep write the sentence "What do I want to dream about tonight?" If you are working on a creative project, spend some time gathering the threads of the problem into your journal before you go to sleep. Who knows, maybe a solution will come to you during the night.

Any spiritual exercise must fit your needs. If these suggestions do not work for you, create your own spiritual exercises. The important thing is to think about your life and to objectify your thinking by writing your thoughts down. If you will routinely perform your spiritual exercises and act upon them, you will live a happier life.

CONCLUSION

When you talk with your wife about a problem you had at work during the day, you are engaging in spiritual exercise—a dialogue (or self-dialogue in the case of journal entries) intended to favorably affect your mental contents. Imagining yourself the star of *EdTV* is a spiritual exercise. In this movie the hero is paid to be the star of a twenty-four-hour television show that is simply the filming of the hero's daily life. Imagine what you would learn about yourself (and about your loathsome habits) if your every move was transmitted live to a television audience! Another spiritual exercise is called the view from above. In this exercise you look at your current situation "from space" or from a year in the future to gain perspective on a current crisis. In the case of current anger, an effective spiritual exercise is to write a vehement letter addressed to the offending party with no intention to send it. The relief afford by this technique is truly amazing. Visualizing how you will handle an anticipated difficult situation in detail is an effective spiritual exercise. Psychologist Nathaniel Branden's sentence stem exercises are spiritual exercises. See his *Art of Living Consciously* (Branden 1999), for example.

Spiritual exercise is the ritualization of conscious living. It is the routine application of thought to your own mental contents with a view to eliminating, changing, improving, or perfecting them. If you practice spiritual exercise, you will improve your chances for happiness in this life.

> *In the next chapter we will outline our philosophy of reason without using the words metaphysics, epistemology, ethics, politics, or aesthetics.*

Chapter 7—Our Philosophy of Reason

Bring in your guide and your teacher. The mind is the guide, but reason is the teacher. They will bring you out of destruction and dangers. —Robinson 1990, p. 381

My philosophy, in essence, is the concept of man as a heroic being, with his own happiness as the moral purpose of his life, with productive achievement as his noblest activity and reason as his only absolute. —Rand 1957, end pages

To act absolutely in conformity with virtue is nothing but acting according to the laws of our own proper nature. But only in so far as we understand do we act. Therefore, to act in conformity with virtue is nothing but acting, living, and preserving our being as reason directs, and doing so from the ground of seeking our own profit. —Spinoza 1954, p. 269–270

Man should not be in the service of society, society should be in the service of man. —Campbell 1991, p. 8

It is not from the benevolence of the butcher, the brewer, or the baker that we expect our dinner, but from their regard to their own interest. —Smith 1970, p. 119

We all have a philosophy, either implicit or explicit. If you have read this far in this book, your philosophy and mine are very similar. In this chapter we will state more fully our philosophy of reason. Readers of novelist-philosopher Ayn Rand will recognize her influence.

Axioms

Have you ever been subjected to another person's incessant repetition of the question "why?" in response to an assertion of yours? I have witnessed this scene in two contexts. One case is that of a child continually asking "why?" in response to a parent's successively more detailed explanations. The other case is that of a college student responding to every effort at explanation or justification of a philosophical proposition by asking "why?" In order to avoid an infinite regression of whys, there must be a starting point at which the question "why?" is meaningless. In fact, there is such a starting point. The starting point is philosophic axioms. Philosophic axioms are basic premises about which you cannot meaningfully ask "why?" and the foundation upon which all proof of higher propositions is based.

Let us consider the basic premises of our philosophy of reason. Close your eyes for a minute.

* * *

Welcome back. What do you see? You see a book. There are three things that you can say about your seeing this book. One is that the book exists. The second thing you can say is that you exist and are capable of perceiving the book. The third thing is that the book is not a squirrel.

The last sentences are examples of the three philosophic axioms of our philosophy: Existence exists. Consciousness exists. And, to exist is to be a particular thing. You cannot "get under" or ask "Why?" about the fact that existence exists. Existence just is. You cannot "get under" or ask "Why?" about the fact that you exist and have consciousness. You do and you know it. You cannot "get under" or ask "Why?" about the fact that to exist is to be one thing and not another. The book you are holding is not a squirrel and you know it. All of these axioms are perceived by you and me directly and are not subject to debate or proof. These three axioms are the basis of all proof. If you ask the question "Why?" my answer is, you know it by your own senses. Furthermore, any question or assertion you make will include your acceptance of these axioms.

Suppose you say, "I disagree with you about your axioms." You have used all of my axioms in your statement. Your statement presupposes the existence two conscious beings—you and me. Your statement presupposes contents of consciousness—your mental state of disagreement and my ideas with which you disagree. Your statement presupposes that the people and things to which you refer are something in particular and not something else—I am me, not you; you are you, not me; and, you are in disagreement with me, not agreement.

Thus, we have identified three axioms:
- Existence exists.
- Consciousness exists.
- The law of identity—to exist is to be something in particular.

COROLLARIES OF AXIOMS

Let us consider three more ideas that are related to the basic axioms, the primacy of existence, the validity of the senses, and volition.

The proposition "existence is primary" emphasizes the fact that consciousness does not create reality. Consciousness means awareness of that which exists. No matter how much you think about it, you cannot turn this book into a squirrel by an act of consciousness. The function of your faculty of awareness is to identify what is. Your consciousness cannot manufacture an alternative reality. You can imagine, but you are not capable of magic. Also, I am not here denying creativity. Certainly, you can, by observing the laws of nature, adapt nature to your needs. People are capable of manipulating existence to create new things.

Our senses are valid. When you look and see this book in your hand, your senses are not deceiving you. The book is not really a squirrel.

The final fundamental idea of our philosophy is the idea of volition. We have free will. We can choose to focus on a subject or not. You cannot "get under" your choice to focus or not. You do or you do not focus. It is your choice. You have direct mental awareness of this phenomenon.

We have identified three corollaries of the axioms:
- Existence has primacy over consciousness.
- Our senses are valid.
- Human beings have volition.

Man's Nature

Our philosophy of reason defines man as the rational animal. Aristotle used this definition. Man's distinctive means of survival is his conceptual consciousness, his mind. The mind is an individual trait.

Conceptual knowledge is not automatic or infallible. Since the mind is volitional, a human being must choose to think in order to exercise his distinctive means of survival, his conceptual consciousness.

We have made these observations about man:
- Man is the rational animal.
- Man's mind is his means of survival.
- The mind is an individual trait.
- The conceptual faculty is not automatic or infallible. It is volitional.

Morality

Morality "is a code of values to guide a person's choices and actions—the choices and actions that determine the purpose and course of his life (Rand 1961, p. 13)." Ethics is a science, the goal of which is the good of man.

Values are that which a person acts to gain and keep. Only *living* entities have values. Only *life* makes values possible. Life is the only end in itself. All other values are means to the ultimate end that is life. For example, it is a value to go to work. However, work is only a means to an end, in part, money. Money is a value. However, money is only a means to an end, products and services. Products and services are of value, but are likewise means to an end, one's life. Life is the ultimate value. Life is an end in itself. All other values are means to that ultimate end, life.

Life is, therefore, the standard of all lesser values. That which sustains life is good. That which is against life is evil. The standard of our morality is man's life.

Man's life includes all of the categories of the activities of your life identified in the life "time" inventory of chapter 3 and more:
- Sleep
- Personal maintenance

- Career
- Television
- Health and fitness
- Art, music, and reading
- Self-improvement and hobbies
- Friends
- Marriage
- Children
- Spiritual exercise
- Planning

Man's means of survival, as we have said, is his conceptual consciousness. The proper functioning of man's conceptual consciousness is called rationality. The functioning of the human consciousness is an individual characteristic. If man is to survive, he must use his conceptual consciousness. He must practice the virtue of rationality. If man is to survive, he must adapt nature to his needs. He must practice the virtue of productivity. If man is to choose life, he must regard himself as worthy and capable of it. He must practice the virtue of pride. The three cardinal values of our morality are reason, purpose, and self-esteem. The corresponding virtues are rationality, productivity, and pride. A virtue is a commitment in mind and action to achieving certain values.

It is apparent from our description of morality that morality is, primarily, a tool to help you to live. Morality is not, primarily, a weapon to condemn others.

We make these statements about morality:
- Morality is necessary in order to live.
- The standard of morality is man's life.
- The cardinal virtues are rationality, productivity, and pride.
- The corresponding values are reason, purpose, and self-esteem.
- Morality is, primarily, a tool to help you to live.
- Morality is not, primarily, a weapon to condemn others.

Man and Society

Man derives enormous benefits from living in society, but only on certain conditions. If man is a beast of burden for a dictator or an all-powerful socialist state, then he is deprived of the use of his functioning mind. Since he is under orders or in a concentration camp, he cannot follow the judgment of his own mind in pursuit of his life, liberty, property, or happiness. Man without rights is deprived of his means of survival. He might survive for a while, just like the Jews did in Nazi Germany (6.3 million murdered) or the peasants in the Ukrainian Soviet Socialist Republic under Stalin (7 million murdered) or the middle class under the Khmer Rouge in Cambodia (2 million murdered).

The conditions of man's survival in society are man's rights: the rights to life, liberty, property, and the pursuit of happiness.

Rights can be violated only in one way, by the initiation of force. Fraud is a type of force.

The only proper way to deal with others is voluntarily by trade, exchanging value for value. The economic system that recognizes voluntary trade as the proper method for human interaction is called capitalism.

We make these statements about man and society:
- Man has the objectively derived and defined rights to life, liberty, property, and the pursuit of happiness.
- Capitalism is the only moral economic system.

Art

Art serves the purpose of bringing to a person's immediate awareness the sense of living in the world as he imagines it should and could be. Human beings have "high and noble goals." The achievement of these goals takes a lifetime. A person needs spiritual rest and refueling from time to time. Art serves this purpose.

We make this statement about art:
- Art reflects the artist's sense of life.

FELLOWSHIP OF REASON

- Art provides emotional and spiritual fuel for achievement of lifetime goals.

That, simply stated, is an outline of our philosophy of reason.

The Fellowship of Reason is a rational moral community founded upon a philosophy of reason and upon the virtues of benevolence. We have just learned the basics of our philosophy of reason. In the next chapter we will explore the virtues of benevolence.

Chapter 8 — The Virtues of Benevolence

> What justifies you in obstinately discovering this difference—the difference between you and someone else—when objectively what is there is *the same*? —Schrödinger 1961

> If your justification for being an angry and alienated person is our philosophy of reason, then think again. —Anonymous

> The choice is not: selfishness or good will among men. The choice is: altruism or good will, benevolence, kindness, love and human brotherhood. —Branden 1962

WHAT IS THE DIFFERENCE?

The Fellowship of Reason is a rational moral community founded upon a philosophy of reason and upon the virtues of benevolence. The crucial difference between the Fellowship of Reason and some other organizations that embrace our philosophy of reason is this—a loving family, good friends, and vital communities are penultimate values for our members. The virtues necessary to acquire and sustain these values are called the virtues of benevolence. The virtues of benevolence are generosity, tolerance, and sensitivity.

LOVING FAMILY, GOOD FRIENDS, VITAL COMMUNITY

A loving family, good friends, and a vital community are objective values. This seemingly uncontroversial proposition is not obvious to some. Let us examine these values.

Most of us are born with a family that includes parents, siblings, grandparents, aunts, uncles, nieces, nephews, cousins, and more. Many of us are lucky enough to have among our unchosen family people that we admire and enjoy being around. Because many of us value our unchosen family, it is appropriate to consider what actions are required of us to maintain these relations.

Most of us, at some point in our lives, also choose a family. We find a suitable mate and marry him or her. Many of us will, at some time in our lives, choose to become parents with our mate. Because we value our chosen family, it is appropriate to consider what actions are required of us to maintain these relations.

Most of us choose to have friends. Friends allow us to experience ourselves as objective entities in the world. The experience is usually positive. Friends manifest character traits we value, for example, good humor, intelligence, integrity, loyalty, and kindness. Best of all our friends like us. Because we value our chosen friends, it is appropriate to consider what actions are required of us to maintain these relations.

The Fellowship of Reason is a community. The summer conference of the Objectivist Center is a community. A moderated e-mail list on the Internet is a community. A church is a community. A local chapter of the Libertarian party is a community. A homeowners' association is a community. A yacht club is a community. A toastmasters club is a community. There are literally thousands of communities to which we can choose to belong. A community is a voluntary group of people united together for a common purpose. Because we value our chosen communities, it is appropriate to consider what actions are required of us to maintain these relations.

Generosity

There may be someone who does not value family, friends, or community. Let us call such a person a truncated individual. He is truncated because he is cut off from the value that most of us find in our relationships with others.

A truncated individual's mother is coming to visit. She calls him to discuss transportation from the airport.

Hi, son. I'm arriving at 5 p.m. tomorrow on WorldAir flight 12. How will I get to your house?

Well, mom, a taxi costs about $25 or you can rent a car for $25 a day. That way you can get around while you're here.

Son, can't you pick me up?

Sure I can. I can even give you a discount from the taxi price. I'll pick you up and return you to the airport for $40.

You're not kidding are you?

Why no, Mom, I'm not. I'm a rational individualist. I don't believe in sacrifice.

Son, I'm your mother.

I know that Mom, but A is A and I can't, as matter of moral conscience, give my valuable time away without compensation. It wouldn't be rational.

I can't believe your father and I raised you to become such a person.

Hey, Mom, you know I love you, but my highest value is me. A is A.

Son, forget it. I'll go visit your sister.

    The truncated son has every legal right to negotiate with his mother for her transportation costs. However, by doing so, he declares that his relationship with his mother is not worth a small investment of his time and the use of his automobile. His mother has every legal and moral right to choose not to visit her son upon learning that he does not value their relationship.

As the conversation above illustrates, generosity is an important virtue in the maintenance of the value of family.

Generosity is the act of giving value (a person's time, effort, work, or property) to an individual or organization without legal right to or expectation of specific immediate return, as an expression of the giver's values.

Examples of generosity among friends include picking up the check at dinner from time to time, picking up your friend's newspapers from her driveway when she is out of town, and the giving of gifts at baby showers, birthdays, graduations, weddings, and anniversaries. No specific immediate return is expected from these acts of generosity, but when your birthday comes along you may hope for a small remembrance yourself. Generosity is just a small part of what friendship is all about. Don't worry, you need not pick up the dinner check to have friends. Going Dutch is an option. Picking up the dinner check is just an example. The specific acts of generosity will vary depending upon the specific circumstances of the relationship.

Examples of generosity with respect to community vary with the community in question. If, for example, you were a member of a small yacht club that owned a clubhouse, you might on occasion respond to the Commodore's call to the members to help with the annual spring cleaning. You need not help every year, but if your clubhouse is to be clean, some members will have to volunteer each year. If the community that is your yacht club is to work, the generosity of the members will be required. You can be a producer or a moocher in your chosen community. If you act to sustain your chosen values, you are acting with integrity. If you fail to act to sustain your chosen values, you lack integrity.

If you value the freedom we enjoy in America, you might choose to give some of your time or money to promote ideas that you believe will help improve our political system. You might choose, for example, to make a donation to a freedom-oriented think tank like the Cato Institute in Washington, D.C. to advance the founding principles of our country. You might even choose to give up a high-paying job in private business to run for public office from which position you could actively promote freedom.

As a member of the community of the family of man, you might choose to give money to a charitable organization to provide disaster relief to a neighboring community badly damaged by tornadoes. You needn't, but if you choose to value the relief of suffering caused by natural disasters, you might give a few dollars from time to time. Obviously, each person will have her own personal generosity budget. The budget might be zero. It is a matter of personal choice. It is a matter of one's chosen values.

Generosity is a virtue that must be practiced at all stages of life to maintain the values of family and friends. However, the degree to which you value your various chosen communities by practicing generosity is a function of the stage of your productive life. Almost all human beings are net creators over the entire span of their lifetimes. By that I mean that most individuals produce more than they consume in their lifetimes. Many individuals produce a great deal more than they consume and I do not refer only to the Andrew Carnegies of the world. (Andrew Carnegie was a great steel industrialist whose philanthropic gifts included 2,509 public libraries.) Any producer who dies leaving property to be inherited by his chosen beneficiaries is obviously a net creator, and that includes most people. Many people who are abundant producers can and do choose to be generous during their lives. They realize that they can afford to reward themselves, their families, and friends with all the material abundance they desire, and still elect to value their chosen communities, including the family of man, by being generous.

Community generosity is a virtue more often practiced by mature individuals who are able to afford it. There are in life an unlimited number of things to value. Because our lives are limited in time and we are limited in our productive ability, we are able to choose only a very limited number of things to value. What we choose to value is, for the most part, morally optional. If we are just starting out in life as young adults, we will not be building libraries for the family of man like Andrew Carnegie. Instead, we will be saving for the down payment on our first house or for our children's college education. Most of us, for lack of productive ability, will never be able to choose to value the family of man to the extent of building libraries. But even were you capable of building libraries, doing so is morally optional. That which you choose to value is, for the most part, your own business.

Generosity is a virtue. Its function is to sustain certain classes of personally chosen values including family, friends, and community.

Tolerance and independence

A good friend is someone with whom you have a great deal in common and with whom you share a common affinity. But, you know, I have never met myself. That is, I have never met a person with whom I have had everything in common: the same political views, the same artistic preferences, the same philosophy, the same *joie de vivre*, etc. Nevertheless, I am fortunate to have some good friends. I have had significant differences of opinion with all of my friends about important philosophical issues. For example, while I am not a theist, many of my closest friends are theists. For another example, I know no one who shares all of my artistic tastes. None of my friends appreciates Salvador Dali, for example. The person most like myself, I suppose, would be my wife. But even she does not appreciate Dali.

The reasons for differences among individual human beings include variations of experience, interest, taste, temperament, intelligence, and talent. Each of us is a work in progress. We all are striving to improve ourselves and working toward perfection, but our work is never complete. We get better and better. But there will always be room for improvement. Furthermore, each of us is working to improve ourselves in different ways at different times at different paces and with varying degrees of success. Today I am working to understand why religion has been important to humankind for millennia. One of my friends is working to improve his golf stroke. Both pursuits are perfectly valid. Since I do not play golf and he is a theist, we generally talk about other matters, for instance, our children.

Another reason for differences among individual human beings is differences of learning. Man's means of survival is his capacity to reason. But reason is not automatic and it is not infallible. The method of reason, logic, is not uniformly taught or widely respected. Most people accumulate their ideas using a combination of tools, among them uncritical acceptance of authoritative lessons, emotions, and reason. That ideas differ widely among people is not surprising.

An important identification of our philosophy of reason is that the faculty of reason, the human mind, is an attribute of the individual. The mind is not a collective entity. Both your mind and my mind are trying to identify the nature of the world and how we can best succeed in it. We want to understand. But because of our various experiences, interests, temperaments, intelligence, talents, learning, commitment to reason, understanding of reason, and fallibility, our mental contents are not identical. The fact that our mental contents are not identical, combined with the recognition that we both want to understand and are of great value to one another, requires that we practice the virtue of tolerance.

Tolerance is the practice of treating other human beings with respect, despite differences among us, in recognition of their value and individuality. Respect means to acknowledge in word and deed another's independence and self-value. A manifestation of tolerance is civility, the practice of being civil to one another.

Some human beings are not trying to identify the nature of the world and instead are trying to avoid knowing it. For some people avoidance of the facts of reality, usually important facts about themselves, is their primary method of functioning. They are often dependent rather than independent. They often exhibit self-hatred rather than self-love. They are not worthy of respect. Such people, often criminals, are a source of evil in the world. Such people are not valuable and may not safely be tolerated. But such people are, fortunately, rare. The important moral criterion is this: Does the other person want to understand? If the person's primary motive of thought is "I want to understand," then his erroneous views should be tolerated. If his primary motive is "I want to avoid knowing," then he should be avoided.

As stated above, every human being makes errors and reaches false conclusions. The penalty for error (for having ideas inconsistent with reality) is that the person holding the false idea suffers or fails in some way. Learning is the usual consequence of failure or suffering, though sometimes serious loss, injury, or even death results. Generally, though, my failure or suffering will not adversely affect you. For example, if I believed in miracles and spent time praying for them, my failure to achieve my goals because of my false idea will not impact you. For another example, if I believe that investing in a fast-food outlet called Martin's Burgers specializing in soybean burgers in Texas beef country is a good idea and lose my investment, my failure to make a profit will not impact you. In short, I must act to sustain my life using my own judgment and suffer the consequences or earn the rewards. My life is, generally, none of your business. In fact, the living of your own life is a full-time job and you will not have the time (if you are looking after your own interests) to live mine. My life is my responsibility. You have no right (unless invited) to tell me how to live. And I would be wrong if I followed your advice, unless I reached my own independent conclusion that your advice was correct. Despite my poor religious or business judgment, we might still be friends, even good friends. Obviously, your appraisal of me will include the opinion that I have bad judgment in some areas. You may wish to avoid taking my advice on problem solving (miracles do not happen) or on investments (soybean burgers do not do well in Texas).

The single greatest problem of some groups that purport to follow our philosophy of reason is the expectation that the acolytes must agree with the adepts or face excommunication from the group. This *false* idea comes from the *truth* that there is only one reality and "A is A." Admittedly, it is vitally important *to me* that *my* ideas be consistent with reality. In fact, to be right is, fundamentally, a matter of life and death, *my* life and death. But for me to be right is important to *me*. Likewise, it is vitally important *to you* that *your* ideas be consistent with reality. If your idea X and my idea X are consistent with reality, they will, naturally, be the same because "A *is* A." However, it is not usually a matter of *your* life and death (or even a matter of great importance) that *my* ideas be consistent with reality. The great irony of this view requiring uniformity of mental contents is that it is completely inconsistent with the virtue of independence, which our philosophy of reason venerates.

An important penalty that an intolerant person suffers is that he removes himself from the family of man, one offended person at a time, thus depriving himself of the values only other human beings can provide. It is a fact that it is rare to have agreement on all ideas among any two people for all the reasons cited above, chief among them commitment to reason, an understanding of reason, and fallibility. We have a long way to go in educating our fellow human beings about the life and death importance of a commitment to reason. If we alienate them, we lose all chance of persuading them to our view and we lose the potential values that they can, as a matter of fact, provide us. Most people are in fact good. Their primary motive of thought is "I want to understand."

Pallas Athena, the daughter of Zeus alone, sprang full-grown and in full armor from Zeus' head. Unlike this ancient Greek goddess, human beings are not born fully grown and fully armed (with knowledge). For human beings, personal moral progress and learning are a life-long process. We are all on different levels within the various subjects of learning. We all specialize in different subjects. At the Fellowship of Reason this fact is recognized and honored in practice by not expecting others to be identical with us in acquired knowledge or taste.

Moral judgment and tolerance

Although tolerance is a virtue, tolerance does not imply that you should befriend or associate with everyone. The most obvious limitation is that even though there may be millions of people who are worthy of your friendship, there just is not enough time in your life to have those relationships. But, more to the point, there are people who will not be valuable to you as friends or associates. These will be good people, but your differences will be too great to form the basis of a friendship. There will be millions more in this category.

If your passionate hobby is riding motorcycles, collecting related riding accessories, and attending motorcycle rallies, then you and I will not likely be friends. Your hobby is completely legitimate. But your and my interests (I enjoy sailing) are not compatible. It is possible, of course, that we may find some other basis for friendship, such as a common interest in ethics. The point is that while you and I value different things (motorcycles and sailboats respectively) we both acknowledge that the other's choice of values is valid *though not shared.*

Tolerance tolerates differences of taste that are not a matter of moral judgment.

Another reason that you might choose not to befriend or associate with another is a difference of ideas. Good people arrive at diverse conclusions about abortion, the death penalty, foreign aid, homosexuality, deployment of military to police the world, gun control, the existence of God, the Welfare State, Social Security, women in the military, smoking, *ad infinitum.* Our philosophy of reason holds that only one side of each argument can be correct. But, because of the complexity of the issues, we generally tolerate an opponent's contrary view. In this context, tolerate means to treat the opponent with respect while clearly and emphatically declaring your contrary opinion. Human beings are fallible. They must exercise their mental faculties volitionally. When issues become complex, the possibility for error increases. Whether you will befriend a person who has reached different conclusions from you on various ideas is a matter of your taste and personal judgment. I have friends who differ with me on any issue in this list. I do not, however, have a single friend who differs with me on every issue. Hope springs eternal and I hope to persuade all of my friends of the errors of their ways or to be persuaded by them.

Although we should tolerate differences of ideas, we need not befriend or associate intimately with those whose ideas are different from our own. Whether you do or not is a matter of your taste and personal judgment. If you err and choose not to associate with an otherwise mostly good person, you may suffer the penalty of not having a friend. If you err and choose to associate with a mostly bad person, you will suffer the penalty of having that friend betray you or otherwise deprive you of value. As with all other choices in your life, you make your judgment, you act upon it, and you suffer the consequences or earn the rewards.

Tolerance tolerates differences of ideas even when those ideas are a matter of moral judgment when your opponent's motive of thought is "I want to understand."

An exception to toleration of bad ideas is the case of a person who is not interested in reason. A person who explicitly chooses to abandon reason as his means of arriving at his ideas is not, obviously, reachable by reason. There are only two ways to deal with other people, reason or force. We have no right to deal with others by force. Reason is not possible by this other person's own choice. Therefore, the only option available is to avoid dealing with the person, at least in his zone of irrationality. You might choose to directly communicate to this person the importance of a commitment to reason. You might succeed in showing the person his choices are to reason or to be shunned. You may not. Again it is a matter of your taste and personal judgment. Avoidance is not toleration.

There are people who are positively distasteful. A man who chooses to dress like a woman, flaunting his faux-female sexuality in sight of your children may be offensive to you. An anarchist flaunting his hate for values that you hold dear (for example by burning or otherwise desecrating the American flag) might be offensive to you. These people should have the legal right to perform these distasteful acts. But you are entitled to shun them, to avoid them, and to show them no tolerance.

There are people who are physically dangerous. Tragically, some people have serious uncontrolled mental illnesses, paranoid schizophrenics or psychopaths for instance. Others are simply criminals. These people do not have the right to threaten or cause injury to others. You should avoid criminals when you can and you should aid, when appropriate, the government to arrest, convict, and punish them. We do not tolerate criminals or the mentally ill when they are a physical threat.

You can and should evaluate other people's moral character. It is an important criterion for choosing your associates and friends. A person who lacks honesty, integrity, pride, rationality, justice, independence, or productivity is not a good candidate for friendship. The reason is that such a person is not safe. You are in danger in the presence of such a person. If he is dependent, he will drain your energies. If he is dishonest, he will steal your property. If he lacks justice, he will betray you. You evaluate another person's moral character in order to enhance your own chances for survival and success.

Moral judgment and tolerance are not inconsistent. You always appraise the moral character of others with whom you have contact. The scales upon which you judge a person's moral character include honesty, integrity, pride, rationality, justice, independence, or productivity. You do not tolerate dishonesty, lack of integrity, an absence of pride, irrationality, injustice, dependence, or lack of productivity. You avoid persons who fail to have these virtues. Tolerance pertains to differences of chosen values by reason of experience, interest, taste, temperament, intelligence, and talent and to differences of complex ideas by reason of learning, commitment to reason, understanding of reason, and fallibility, where your opponents primary motive of thought is "I want to understand."

Sensitivity

Practicing the virtue of sensitivity will enhance your candidacy for a loving family, good friends, and vital communities.

Sensitivity is the application of the principle "I want to understand" to other people. If you want to understand another, you will regard him closely, consider his words and actions, and attempt to understand his motivations and to divine his intentions. You will communicate your understanding and appreciation of him. When you find him to be of value, you will befriend him.

Sensitivity is crucial for the creation and maintenance of a loving family, good friends, and vital communities.

You find yourself in a university class on the first day of fall semester. You notice that a fellow student, a young lady, is looking at you. When your eye catches hers she does not turn away, but looks at you confidently and smiles. You are the first to turn away, returning your attention to the class. Your classmate has communicated to you unmistakably "I want to know you." After class you approach her and introduce yourself. In the days ahead, you learn about her. She learns about you. You discover that you have many things in common, including a common interest in rational individualism. You find that you are powerfully drawn to one another sexually. You become lovers.

Sensitivity is one of the most important virtues in locating and keeping a mate and friends generally.

You have an interest in boating and you notice a small ad for a yacht club in the newspaper. You call the number and are invited to attend a meeting next week. When you arrive no one speaks to you. Everyone seems to know one another. There are several small groups of friends chatting. You approach one small group to introduce yourself. The group seems discomforted by your presence and slightly annoyed that their conversation has been interrupted. You move away from the group and slip out the door. Next year you are not surprised to learn that the yacht club has closed its doors for lack of membership.

Communities cannot survive without the virtue of sensitivity. The members of a vital community must constantly be on the lookout for new members. The focused light of your attention must be directed toward potential new members of the community. You must communicate the idea "I want to know you" in order to create and nurture communities.

THE PENALTY FOR LACKING VIRTUE

The cardinal virtues are rationality, productivity, and pride. Other important virtues are honesty, integrity, justice, and independence. In this chapter we have identified the virtues of benevolence: generosity, tolerance, and sensitivity.

What is the penalty for lacking these virtues?

There are only two ways of dealing with others: force and reason. Force is prohibited. When reason is excluded because the other is irrational, the only remaining option is not to deal with the other. You avoid him.

A person who lacks productivity cannot support himself and must survive by theft or by handouts. In either case, you avoid him. A person who lacks pride, self-love, is incapable of valuing others. You avoid him. A person who is dishonest, lacks integrity, commits injustice, or is dependent, is a threat to you and yours. You avoid him. A person who lacks generosity may not be a positive threat to you. He evidently does not value a loving family, good friends, or vital communities. You need not avoid him for your personal safety. However, you will not elect to seek him out. If he is of immense value, for example, if he is a genius or other great producer of wealth and value from which you can benefit, his abundant productivity may outweigh his lack of generosity.

You can choose not to value a loving family, good friends, and vital communities. You can be a hermit. In a particular individual case, this choice may be rational or irrational. It depends upon the circumstances. As an observer of a stranger, I am generally not in a position to evaluate the stranger's choice to be a hermit. Furthermore, another's decision not to value a loving family, good friends, and vital communities is of no interest to me. The point is that neither you nor I will choose to seek out a hermit to form relationships (family, friendship, or community). The situation is analogous to a group whose uniting principle is gun control. Such a group will not spend money soliciting for new members using the mailing list of the National Rifle Association. The two groups' values are diametrically opposed. People with different values do not generally associate with one another. Those who do not value a loving family, good friends, and vital communities will not have them.

In short, the penalty for lacking the virtue of generosity is that others who value loving families, good friends, and vital comminutes will not seek you out as a candidate for more or less intimate relationships, unless you possess other extraordinary virtues of overriding importance.

A person who lacks tolerance is a person who refuses to recognize your independence and self-value. He communicates his opinion that you are worthless or evil. He wants conformity to his views, not based upon reason, but upon threat of his moral disapprobation. He chooses to deal with you not based upon reason, but by your fear of not being liked by him. Such people are not sources of value. You avoid intolerant people.

A person who lacks sensitivity fails to communicate "I want to know you." There are so many values in the world to choose from it is likely that you will skip the opportunity to deal with an insensitive person. Human beings are value seekers.

HUMAN BROTHERHOOD AND THE FAMILY OF MAN

The individual human being is sacred. (In this discussion, sacred means of the highest value.) This proposition is the essence of rational individualism. For each individual his own life is his own highest value. But I wish to say more than this. I wish to say that other individual human beings are sacred to each of us. The reason is that the individual human being is the source of all human values. As the source of *all* values, the individual is sacred to each of us.

The adult individual takes the undifferentiated material of existence, molds it in the pattern of his thought, and creates values, not *ex nihilo*, but from himself and from the material of existence. Everything we value from bricks to books, from mustard to music, from friends to family, is a product of individual human effort.

In a political climate in which human beings are not able to exploit each other by legal or illegal means, other people are unqualifiedly valuable and essential to our personal happiness. Other human beings are not optional values. Most of us would not choose to be hermits. Even Robinson Crusoe had his Friday. This is not to say that you cannot imagine a world (like Hitler's Germany) populated by people so evil that living is all but impossible, but we do not live in such a world today.

Individual human happiness is only achievable among other human beings. (If all other human beings were evil, then individual human happiness would not be possible.) Without other human beings, we could not experience psychological visibility. There would be no others to react to us. Without other human beings, all jobs and careers available in society cease to exist. There would be no one with whom to trade. What is the use of a writer without someone to read his book? What is the use of an insurance salesman without someone to insure? We must have good relationships with other human beings in order to be happy.

It is a fact that individual human beings are the source of all human values and that human beings require good relationships with others. This fact forms the basis of what I have called the family of man and is the basis of a general feeling of human brotherhood.

Emergency Aid

My first reaction to considering the question of the explicit moral basis for rendering aid in emergencies is that the question is only of philosophic interest. Obviously, everyone would help a person in a life-threatening emergency if he could without serious risk to his own life, and some would help even in the face of death. I am not here thinking of professional fire fighters and the like, but of civilian bystanders. However, upon reflection, I realized that the question is not simply of philosophic interest. In 1963, Kitty Genovese was murdered near her apartment in Queens while several of her neighbors listened and watched from their windows but did nothing. During and prior to the Second World War, many people failed to help Jewish people hide or escape from the Nazis. Many actually cooperated with the Nazis.

It is claimed that heroic bystanders and rescuers of Jews are the heart of altruism (Monroe 1996). If I am to successfully claim that our philosophy of reason is correct and that the morality of altruism is erroneous, I must account for the moral excellence of heroic bystanders and rescuers of Jews or any victim of totalitarianism.

A heroic bystander is a person who happens to witness a situation that immediately threatens the life of another, but not the life of the bystander. A young girl is the victim of an attempted rape. The bystander is a neighbor who sees the attack outside her apartment window. Or, a non-swimming child falls into a river. The bystander is a nearby picnicker who hears the drowning child's screams for help. The bystander is physically capable of intervening and has some chance of success. The neighbor witnessing the attempted rape is not, for example, confined to a wheelchair, and is in good physical condition. The picnicker witnessing the drowning child knows how to swim. However, the bystander will risk his own life if he intervenes. The witness to the rape might herself be raped or killed upon confronting the rapist. The witness to the drowning might drown in her attempt to save the child.

The rescuer of Jews is a person who, during the Nazi persecution and extermination of the Jews, hid a Jewish person from the Nazis or helped a Jewish person escape the Nazis.

Conventional morality asserts that a person has a moral duty to help others and that to withhold that aid is a moral fault. "So in everything, do to others what you would have them do to you, for this sums up the Law and the Prophets (Matthew 7:12)." Our philosophy of reason says that life is the standard of value and that your life is your own proper purpose. Our philosophy does not recognize divinely imposed duties. So what is our philosophic rationale for recognizing that the heroic bystander and the rescuer of Jews are supremely moral beings?

A human being is an integrated being of body and mind. Both physical and psychological survival are necessary. Sometimes, tragically, an individual has to choose between physical and psychological survival. Heroes choose psychological survival. Those who choose physical survival suffer possibly irreparable psychological damage.

Psychological survival has three components—the sense that life is worth living, the sense that one is worthy of living, and the sense that one is capable of living.

All three components of psychological survival are threatened by the situations in which the heroic bystander and the rescuer of Jews find themselves.

The sense that life is worth living

A world dominated by Nazis or violent criminals is not a world in which life is worth living. Fortunately, Nazis and criminals do not dominate the world in which we live. Generally speaking, western civilization, the United States of America in particular, is the environment suitable to man's nature as a producer and trader of values. Political freedom is the rule in the West, rather than the exception. In a free society human beings are free to make judgments about how best to live and flourish, and to implement those judgments in action. Everyone is free to enter into voluntary relationships with others for commerce, social intercourse, and intimate relations. Everyone is free not to relate with others, should he wish. Only violence and fraud are prohibited.

Human beings cannot survive well in slavery or while subject to random violence. The Dark Ages were dark because human beings who produced values risked their lives by doing so. Subject to raids by barbarians (peoples who lived by looting, enslaving, and killing others), the only way to survive, if at all, was to reduce one's production, including personal hygiene, to bare subsistence levels so that there was nothing to steal. All values, including physical beauty and intelligence, were best hidden from the looters.

Nazis and violent criminals will kill unless restrained. Because there are and were heroic bystanders and rescuers of Jews (to say nothing of the Allies and the police), Nazis and violent criminals do not dominate our world today.

Every civilized human being with a modicum of education understands that evil must be resisted in order to function as a human being, as a producer and trader. Freedom is necessary for human life. Freedom is the presence of the rights to life, liberty, the pursuit of happiness, and property. Freedom is the absence of slavery and random violence.

For us who have seen the peak of human civilization, returning to the Dark Ages is not an option. Therefore, civilized human beings fight Nazis and violent criminals, sometimes to the death.

FELLOWSHIP OF REASON

The sense that one is worth living

The mythological ring of Gyges renders its wearer invisible. In the myth the possessor of the ring used it to kill the reigning king of Lydia and usurp his throne. Imagine for the purpose of this argument that our witnesses to the rape and the drowning are each wearing such a ring. Neither witness will suffer public humiliation for not helping the rape victim or the drowning child. Should they allow the rape to proceed or the child to drown, nobody will know. Each witness is invisible. Only the witness himself will know.

It is a fact that human beings are the source of all values. Everything that we value as human beings is either an actual human being or the product of human beings. Even a beautiful sunset is, in a sense, the product of human beings, because one's very existence and the time and freedom for leisure are human products.

A human being's sense of worth comes from his conviction that he is a source of values. To be a source of values means to create new values, or to preserve and maintain existing values. The opposite is to be a destroyer of values.

There is only one sacred thing on earth and that is the individual human being. Each individual human being is supremely valuable to himself and very often to at least some others, for instance, his parents. Generally, the world is auspicious for the survival of human beings. Sometimes, in an emergency, the actual circumstances in which an individual finds himself are not auspicious for survival. In emergency circumstances, a sacred human being may need outside assistance to survive. Everyone is subject to exceptions to the rule that reality is auspicious for human survival.

Our witness wearing the ring of Gyges can either stop the rapist and allow the child to drown, or she can risk her life to save them. Because she is wearing the ring of Gyges, no one else will know of her choice. What will she do?

There is no difference in principle between you and me. We are both sacred human beings. Our witness, likewise, knows that there is no difference in principle between her and the victim she is watching. Our witness knows that a sacred value is at risk. Our witness's sense of self-worth is now also at risk. Is our witness a creator and preserver of value or is she a destroyer of value?

Fortunately, our witness is a creator and preserver of value. She leaves her apartment and kicks the rapist in the butt, chasing him off. She helps the victim into the witness's apartment and calls the police. When the police catch a suspect, she and the victim identify the rapist. The rapist gets life in prison.

Our drowning witness runs down the bank of the river ahead of the thrashing child. He jumps in and pulls the child to safety.

Our rescuer of Jews takes in the Jewish child and hides the child in her basement until the war is over.

The sense that one is capable of living

Healthy human beings do not enjoy feeling like helpless victims. They enjoy a sense of efficacy. When barbarians (be they Nazis or violent criminals) roam, one must protect oneself against them. The fact that a stranger happens to be the present victim of the Nazis or the criminal in no way reduces the threat posed by barbarians. In order to sense that one is capable of living, one must *be* capable of living and that includes taking out the bad guys when one can.

Summary on emergency aid

If the individual is to survive, he must look to both his physical and psychological survival. Sometimes one must risk physical survival to ensure psychological survival. Sometimes a person's values dictate that he must give up his life entirely for his values, though this happens very rarely in real life.

Heroic bystanders and rescuers of Jews are supremely moral beings according to our philosophy of reason. But the reason is not that they have complied with a divine duty, the reason is that they achieve their own values, including specifically their own psychological survival, by their heroic deeds.

Empathy as a Root of the Virtues of Benevolence

All normal people experience empathy. A person completely lacking in empathy is a sociopath. The factual basis of empathy is the firm knowledge of our common humanity. There are no fundamental physical differences between you and me, only differences of measurement. I am six feet, one inch tall. You are five feet, two inches tall, or whatever. There are no fundamental psychological differences. You and I experience the same types of emotions and thoughts. We are siblings. In all probability we literally have a common ancestor. We are made of the same stuff—star dust, in fact.

The only difference between you and me is in our perspective. I am *this* mind-body in *my* life circumstances. You are *that* mind-body in *your* life circumstances. I have my life to live. You have your life to live. I am the proper beneficiary of my own actions. You are the proper beneficiary of your own actions. We each recognize that the other is an end in himself.

When I hear of another human being's faultless suffering, his suffering can be as real to me as my own *imagined* suffering in the same circumstances. I hesitate to give examples because of the psychic pain involved. I will choose a benign case. Imagine your friend, a co-worker, comes into the office to announce her discovery that all four tires of her car have been stabbed with a knife and flattened in the office parking lot. Not only will you experience distress at her loss, you will rush out in a panic to your own car to make sure that it has not suffered similar vandalism.

The reason for my compassion for my co-worker (compassion derives from Latin roots meaning "to suffer with") is that I identify myself with her. I can imagine exactly what she must be feeling at her loss. Because my co-worker in no way caused her loss, I can easily picture myself in her place.

Naturally, I do not feel the actual pain of my co-worker's suffering. My *awareness* of her suffering and my own *imagined* suffering in the same circumstances are only ideas in my head, but these *ideas* are practically identical.

This empathic identification with others is a psychological basis for the virtues of benevolence. These virtues are not equivalent to altruism.

Altruism's Mistakes

Rational individualism and altruism are philosophical opposites. Individualism is the view that you have a moral right to live for your own sake. Altruism is the view that you do not have a right to live for your own sake and that service to others is the justification of your existence. Our philosophy of reason is individualistic. We reject altruism. Ayn Rand's *Atlas Shrugged* is a one-thousand-page polemic against altruism.

One psychological basis of altruism is empathy. Because the virtue of benevolence and the vice of altruism share a common psychological root, they are often confused. A popular beneficiary of altruism is the homeless person.

(Let me make it clear that helping a homeless person can be both an altruistic action and a rationally individualistic action. The difference is in the actor's motive.)

The empathic altruist sees a homeless person and feels painful empathy saying to himself, "There but for the grace of God go I." He is motivated to help.

The altruist's number one mistake is allowing his empathic desire to help others to become a conviction that he has the right to force other people to fulfill his private desire to help. When the altruist acts to force others, he becomes a criminal. When an altruist votes to have the government forcibly take money from others (by taxation) to pay for government programs to "help" the homeless, he is violating the rights of others. It is *not* a violation of the rights of others for the altruist to buy the homeless person a bowl of soup or to set up a charitable foundation to receive voluntary contributions and give aid to the homeless.

Another altruist mistake is misidentifying what human life is all about. Human life is not about surviving like a stray dog on scraps from a garbage can. Human life is about acting to achieve your goals. No one can help another person do this. If you support a person in his decision to live like a stray dog and to avoid living like a human being, you are *not* helping him in any human sense.

Another altruist mistake is acting as a barrier between reality and bad judgment. If a person were on a desert island and he failed to create the values required to live (food and shelter), he would die. On a desert island, there is no one there to help you avoid the fact of reality that you must produce in order to consume. Living in a wealthy, modern society among producers, it is possible to avoid the consequences of failing to create the values required to live. But avoidance is possible only by stealing the values created by producers or by being given alms. The indiscriminate giving of alms sets up reverse incentives. It can actually create a market for beggars. It can *pay* to be a beggar. No longer are some people motivated to produce the values their lives require. Instead, they are motivated to beg those values from others.

The last of the altruists' mistakes to be mentioned is misidentifying a faultless human being in an emergency situation. This misidentification leads to the false conclusion that people are morally obligated to help the homeless. There are four categories of homeless person that I can think of:

1. *The Con Man*—The professional panhandler is one who chooses to live off of other people's deluded generosity. This person chooses homelessness (or the appearance of homelessness or other desperate need) as a lifestyle. To fake a personal handicap or misfortune is just a little fraud. There is, however, a horrific crime committed for the same motive. The comprachicos were a nomadic association of people in the seventeenth century who bought children and surgically mutilated them to turn them into freaks. The surgically deformed children were then sold for use as beggars. Giving alms makes it possible for this kind of crime to exist. I saw a story in August 1998, originating with the BBC, entitled "'Rat children' beg near shrine." Children in Pakistan, according to the story, are being intentionally deformed at birth for use as very effective beggars before religious shrines. Personally, I prefer not to participate in such a market, whether it be the con man on my street corner or a more extreme version.

2. *The Suicidal Individual*—The self-loathing homeless person is one who is committing suicide very slowly. There are people who have committed undiscovered crimes. Some of these criminals cannot live with themselves. So they give up living. An unprosecuted war criminal is an example. I knew of a person whose misdeeds indirectly caused another's death. He suffered an inconsolable guilt. He slowly killed himself over several years. I personally choose not to support a self-condemned criminal committing slow suicide.

3. *The Chronically Mentally Ill Person*—The chronically mentally ill homeless person may be incapable of producing the values required to live. We each have a *limited budget* for our own generosity. When you set up your personal generosity budget (it might be zero), you will support your own *personal* values (a homeless shelter, a battered women's shelter, the local chapter of the Society for the Prevention of Cruelty to Animals, a recycling center, or a thousand and one other proper beneficiaries for private charity). While there is nothing morally wrong with supporting such a person, there is no moral requirement to do so.

4. *The Person Fallen on Bad Times*—The homeless person who has suffered a misfortune may be temporarily in desperate need. Again, there is nothing wrong with helping another human being in distress. It is not, however, your moral obligation to do so unless the person is the innocent victim of a life-threatening emergency.

Although the emotion of empathy can lead to altruism, it does so erroneously. Altruists are mistaken about the nature of human life—life is about acting to achieve your goals. Altruists are wrong to place their lives and fortunes between people with bad judgment and the consequences of their actions. Altruists are wrong to support professional panhandlers and suicidal criminals. Altruists become criminals when they act to violate the individual rights of others. Altruism, which holds that you do not have the right to live for your own sake, is an inversion of morality. Morality is about living your *own* life well.

Benevolence and Trading Partners

Human beings do not live on desert islands. Human beings live in societies. We receive great benefits from living in societies that respect an individual's rights to life, liberty, property, and the pursuit of happiness. Among other producers, we are able to trade our values for theirs. We receive advantages from competition, economies of scale, and the division of labor.

Human beings are the source of all values. Look around you now: unless you are reading outside, there is nothing about you that is not man-made. Even if you are reading outside, the out-of-doors environment in which you are sitting was very likely molded in its present pleasant arrangement by human beings.

In order to obtain values from other people, you and I must practice the virtues of benevolence.

"Benevolence is a commitment to achieving the values derivable from life with other people in society, by treating them as potential trading partners, recognizing their humanity, independence, and individuality, and the harmony between their interests and ours (Kelley 1996, p. 30)."

Conclusion

The Fellowship of Reason as an institution is unique in that it explicitly unites our philosophy of reason with the virtues of benevolence. Our mottoes for living are "I want to understand," which expresses in one sentence the motive of our philosophy of reason, and "human beings are the source of all human values," which expresses our motive for benevolence.

We have learned enough for now about our philosophy of reason and the virtues of benevolence. In the next chapter, I will talk about Celebration in the Fellowship of Reason. We celebrate our lives, our freedom, and our philosophy of reason.

Chapter 9 — Celebration

> [I]t is the active exercise of our faculties in conformity with virtue that causes happiness. —Aristotle 1934, p. 51

> O my soul; will you ever be good and simple; one and naked; more luminous than the body which surrounds you? Will you ever be fulfilled, without need, neither regretting nor desiring anything? ... Will you ever be happy with what is happening to you at the present moment? —Marcus Aurelius quoted in Hadot 1998, pp. 274–275

> [T]he information we allow into consciousness becomes extremely important; it is, in fact, what determines the content and the quality of life. —Csikszentmihalyi 1991, p. 30

> [T]he kingdom of heaven is near. —Matthew 4:17

INTRODUCTION

The Fellowship of Reason is a rational moral community founded upon a philosophy of reason and the virtue of benevolence. Our common goal is happiness on earth. Our common means to achieving happiness is reason. Our regular meeting is called Celebration.

Happiness requires three activities:

- Virtuous action
- Inner work
- Selective focus of attention

The science of ethics teaches the elements of virtuous action. Inner work or spiritual exercise is the process of becoming aware of the contents of one's consciousness and resolving sources of pain, fear, and guilt.

Celebration is a ritual that leads us to selectively focus our attention upon the good things in life.

DISCIPLINE AND RITUAL

In order to be happy a person must first and foremost identify those things in his life about which he should be happy. A person can discipline himself to attend to the good things in his life and everyone should do so. A person may also seek help in disciplining himself. A runner may join a track club to participate in running events. A pianist may take private lessons to encourage practice. A fitness buff may hire a personal trainer to guide her exercise routine. An overweight person may join a weight-loss organization to find support and encouragement. A person interested in making personal moral progress may join a moral community. People frequently seek outside help to discipline themselves. A rational moral community exists in order to assist its members to discipline themselves to achieve happiness. When an institution imposes a discipline it becomes a ritual. Celebration in the Fellowship of Reason is a ritual.

SELECTIVE FOCUS OF ATTENTION

If you watch local television news in the evening you will see stories about homicide, child abuse, freeway pileups, a product recall, and a scandal involving a local celebrity, plus local weather and sports. Unless you enjoy baseball or are planning a trip and need to know the weather, local television news contributes nothing to your happiness.

If you watch the national news you will see stories about tyrants and warlords murdering each other and their subjects, governments mucking up their economies with anti-freedom polices, politicians demagoguing their constituents, and natural disasters. Unless you are prepared to advocate the colonization of the countries suffering under tyrannies, warlords, or socialist governments, do not waste your time.

If not the wickedness, stupidity, and consequent suffering of other to what *should* one attend in order to achieve happiness? How freedom, visitors, each other, the daily successes of our lives, art, heroes, amateur talent, ethics, personal mission, and reflection for starters?

Celebration of freedom

The regular meeting of the Fellowship of Reason is divided into ten elements. Each element is performed by a volunteer member.

Freedom is the political condition in which the individual rights to life, liberty, the pursuit of happiness, and property are enforced. I would not have been permitted to publish this book during the Inquisition. Human beings cannot produce abundantly and save in the absence of freedom. Life for a slave is "solitary, poor, nasty, brutish, and short." Freedom is the precondition for man's full use of his means of survival—his reasoning mind—and therefore the precondition of health and happiness. The Dark Ages were dark because human beings were not free, but rather subject to random looting and murder by barbarians. Therefore, the first thing we celebrate in the Fellowship of Reason is freedom.

One can celebrate freedom as simply as by reciting the "Pledge of Allegiance to the Flag" or by reading the *Declaration of Independence*. Any activity that calls the attention of our members to the freedom we enjoy is sufficient.

Freedom and, therefore, politics are legitimate concerns for rational individualists. The American regime is the best political system ever created by man. If our constitutional republic is to continue, rational individualists must, voluntarily, contribute their time and money to the preservation of our regime. Although the Fellowship of Reason is not a political organization and eschews political participation, our philosophy of reason regards the political participation of individuals as a virtue, specifically the virtue of generosity. At a minimum, individuals who value freedom should provide financial support to freedom-oriented organizations and candidates, and they should vote.

Celebration of visitors

We are, after all, a fellowship. In order to grow, we must communicate to our guests, "I want to know you." We must practice the virtue of sensitivity.

Other people are mirrors to our own souls. Human beings are the source of all values. We must seek them out if we are to be happy.

Celebration of each other

Given the little attention that is paid to the art of friendship, it seems a miracle that people have any friends at all. "[F]riendships rarely happen by chance: one must cultivate them as assiduously as one must cultivate a job or a family (Csikszentmihalyi 1991, p. 190)."

As a ritual acknowledgment of the importance of friendship, we take a moment during Celebration to greet one another.

Celebratory announcements

Most people's lives are chock full of wonderful events that should be treasured. Few people recognize the value of bringing these occurrences to mind and savoring them. You got an "A" on your mid-term exam. Your dog got lost, but she found her way home unharmed. You celebrated your birthday or your anniversary. You closed on your new house. It's a beautiful day. You won $50 in the lottery. Not a day of your life goes by without many wonderful things happening to you.

The person who does not appreciate the good things, large and small, in his life will not, and is not entitled to, achieve happiness. The ancient name for this sin is acedia. Acedia means spiritual sloth.

To encourage our members to practice the virtue of gratitude, we call upon volunteers to share their celebratory announcements.

Celebration of art

I talked about the importance of art in chapter 1. I suggested that art provides spiritual fuel for an individual's life journey. Celebration of art might be the reading of a member's favorite poem, the viewing of a painting or sculpture, or any similar activity as determined by the volunteer presenter.

Celebration of heroes

Ethics answers the question, "How am I to live?" The science of ethics is large and complex. Applying ethical principles while in the middle of a crisis can be quite difficult. Heroes, though, are concrete embodiments of our ethical principles. Rather than doing a logical analysis that may be impractical "on the ground," one can imagine his or her hero in the same circumstances and picture the proper response to the crisis. Heroes are extremely important in our philosophy of reason.

"My philosophy, in essence, is the concept of man as a heroic being, with his own happiness as the moral purpose of his life, with productive achievement as his noblest activity, and reason as his only absolute (Rand 1957, end pages)."

Celebration of amateur talent

Each of us has some talent. We play the piano, the guitar, or the flute. We can dance or sing. Anybody can read a poem. During each Celebration we enjoy a volunteer member's presentation of his or her talent.

Oratory

The centerpiece of Celebration is a short talk about ethics. We are, after all, a *moral* community.

Topics can be drawn from mythology, religion, philosophy, or everyday life. Plutarch (50–120), for example, wrote essays on talkativeness, bashfulness, marriage, consolations, and against borrowing money. All of the virtues and vices of man are proper subjects. Talks on etiquette are, in my experience, desperately needed. (I recently noticed a couple dining tête-à-tête in a restaurant. Both were talking on their cellular telephones to other people!) Examples of heroes provide wonderful material for oratory. The possible subjects are endless. The goal of oratory is to provide material from any source with which members may make personal moral progress.

Celebration of personal mission

In order to be happy, a person must have a mission in life. The mission should be the actualization of his innate potential excellence, his daemon, or his destiny as discussed in chapter 4. This element of Celebration reminds us of this crucial component of happiness.

Reflection, mindful meditations, or spiritual exercise

In order to be happy, a person must look after his inner state. We call this inner work. Engaging in a mindful meditation during Celebration reminds us of this fact.

Glass is half-full as philosophic principle

Except in the rarest of circumstances, happiness is near at hand. We need only avail ourselves of it. There are people in the world who only attend to the bad things in life. These people can never be happy. Happiness is a state of mind. If your goal is happiness, then you must acknowledge and celebrate the good things in your life. You must act to improve the bad.

EMOTIONAL GOALS OF CELEBRATION

What is sacred to you?

Members of the Fellowship of Reason do not deny, fear, or repress emotions, even powerful emotions. The logic-driven, emotion-repressing Mr. Spock from the original *Star Trek* television series is not a role model. Members of the Fellowship of Reason actively pursue happiness.

Celebration is not primarily an intellectual activity, though it has intellectual components and content. Celebration is an experience designed to elicit an emotional response. The goals of Celebration are spiritual. (Spiritual in this case means of or pertaining to consciousness.)

Because members of the Fellowship of Reason want to understand explicitly, not merely intuitively, we will learn now the specific emotional goals of Celebration.

There are several emotional states that we seek to create directly. Once those states are achieved (all good in themselves), a final emotional reward will on some occasions and for some members be achieved.

- Tranquility (safety and peace): Celebration is ritualistic, that is, it proceeds according to a pattern. It starts on time and it ends on time. Each Celebration has the same elements (celebration of freedom, visitors, each other, announcements, etc.) in a regular order. One purpose of this ritual is to put the minds of those attending Celebration at ease. Surprise, expectation, and wonder about what will happen next (all good things in a proper context) are not conducive to tranquility and introspection.

- Self-esteem: Celebration is a moral experience. The purpose of morality is to teach you to enjoy yourself and live. We are intensely alive during Celebration. We enjoy ourselves during Celebration. Furthermore, an explicit intellectual purpose of Celebration is to teach morality. In sum, it is crucial that those attending Celebration feel that they are in a good place and feel good about themselves for being there.

- Trust: To allow another person to intentionally elicit an emotional response from you is an act of intimacy. For this to be possible, the members must trust the performers of Celebration. Allowing yourself to experience powerful emotions in the presence of others is also an act of intimacy. Those present during Celebration must trust one another. Building trust requires time and commitment by the members.

- Introspection: An emotional response in each of those attending Celebration is our goal. Each person attending Celebration must be focused upon her own mental state and upon her own mental contents. She can use the explanation in this section to guide herself toward those preliminary emotional states. Our mindful meditation presents an opportunity for the members to look inward.

- Freedom from daily cares: Members must by act of conscious will put aside thoughts of yesterday and tomorrow. One goal of Celebration is to achieve what I call in chapter 12 a "now moment." The "now" cannot be fully experienced while obsessing about the past or worrying about the future. Ideally, Celebration will occur in a "Temple of the Human Spirit." The design of such a place will direct the mind toward the eternal contents of one's own soul and away from daily cares.

- Reverence: Worship, honor, sacred, hero, reverence, consecrate, holy, glorious—we want to hold these words, and more precisely the people, ideas, and objects with which we associate these words, in our minds during Celebration. Until my wife and I had our first child, I did not understand what the word "worship" meant. Now I do. You, dear reader, have your own sacred values. We are connected during Celebration with our highest values. Our highest values are necessarily intensely personal, but candidates include yourself, your spouse or life partner, your children, your career, your parents, your hero, your friend, a loved one, your sacred space or object (such as the writer's working place, the artist's easel, the sculptor's clay, or the musician's instrument), the creative ability of man, and the heroic potential of man. These are the things to which we turn our attention during Celebration.

- Aesthetic awareness: During Celebration we experience musical, poetic, and artistic performances. We enjoy aesthetic experiences. Our artistic senses are turned on. We experience, through art, an immediate experience of our own sense of life.

Now when all of these elements are present (tranquility, self-esteem, trust, introspection, freedom from daily cares, reverence, and aesthetic awareness) we are ready to receive our final emotional reward—the rapture of being alive.

If you have ever had this experience you will know that it is a profound one worth experiencing. The experience involves an intense awareness of and reverence for yourself. The experience often includes a sense that you are in your proper place in the universe, that you belong and are rooted to where you are.

The experience is the aesthetic appreciation of that work of art (you are the artist) that is your own self and life in your own setting, your particular place in the world. This is the experience I call "sacred being."

> *In the next chapter we will discover the rational rituals of the Fellowship of Reason.*

Chapter 10—Rational Rituals

Bad parenting is the root of all evil. —Anonymous

Yes, there is a "secret to happiness"—and it is gratitude. All happy people are grateful, and ungrateful people *cannot* be happy. —Prager 1999, p. 59

We're so engaged in doing things to achieve purposes of outer value that we forget that the inner value, the rapture associated with being alive, is what it's all about. —Campbell 1991, p. 5

LIFE IS PRECIOUS

Imagine that all scientists of the world conclude with certainty that our sun will supernova in a month. You learn that the explosion will disintegrate your body in a microsecond and that your nervous system will not have time to register pain. You will simply cease to exist thirty days hence at noon Eastern Standard Time. There is nothing to do. Even if you had access to a space shuttle, there is nowhere to go. The explosion of the sun will turn the entire solar system into elementary particles at nearly the speed of light.

After the initial shock and a reasonable attempt to verify the scientific conclusions, eventually you accept your certain end. The next morning you walk out into a beautiful, clear spring morning. The sun is shining brightly and there is a light breeze. You notice the smell of spring flowers. You walk into your herb garden. You pick a mint leaf, crush it between your fingers, and smell the fragrance. You feel the warm sun on your neck. You look up to see your children come bursting out of the house on a rush of energy to play on the swings. You see your wife looking lovingly after them from the back door. You look at your house. No, you look at your *home*. You are proud of it. It is your dream home and you were able to make that dream come true. All of these things, your garden, your mint, this day, the children, your wife, your home, you suddenly realize *are* you. They are *your* values. Things you have wanted, chosen, and achieved. Things you have conceived and nurtured. These things are precious. You kneel on the ground in your garden and push your fingers up to your palms in the cool, damp earth. You make fists as if to grab the whole of the earth and hold it to yourself. God, you love this life.

Well, scientists have not concluded that the sun will supernova in a month. Nevertheless, it is certain that you will simply cease to exist some days (hopefully a great many) hence. Your life is precious whether it is to end in thirty days or in thirty years. Revere your own life now and every day of your life.

The rational rituals described below will help you maintain an attitude of deep gratitude, respect, and awe toward your life.

STAGES OF LIFE

There are several important transitions and stages in the life of man: birth, the transition from infancy to childhood, puberty, adolescence, young adulthood, marriage, parenthood, midlife, menopause, retirement, old age, and death. The Fellowship of Reason celebrates many of these stages and transitions.

Celebrations of pregnancy and birth

We make many important and permanent choices in life. The choice of career, the choice of spouse, and the choice to have children are among the most important.

"Keep your options open" is a saying I grew up with. The high divorce rate and the high rate of one-parent families during the last thirty years of the twentieth century suggest many people applied the saying to the choice of spouse and children. This application is an error. Marriage and children are NOT about "keeping your options open."

"Keep your options open" should be an admonition directed to children and adolescents about the realm of adult choices. It means that before your make an important choice, be sure you have fully informed yourself of all relevant options. Be ready to make, from among them, a permanent and final selection. Once any choice is made, there *are* consequences and many of those consequences are permanent and final.

The most permanent choice you can make is to choose to have children. An infant requires constant attention for years. A youngster must be nurtured and educated for upwards of eighteen years. The parents who create a child are, and have chosen to be, responsible to perform this task involving almost two decades.

Therefore, when a woman chooses to become pregnant, she and her husband have embarked on one of the greatest adventures life has to offer. They have left their life as a childless couple behind. They will not return to that life, if ever, until after the passage of at least twenty years, one-third of an adult lifetime.

We of the Fellowship of Reason celebrate pregnancy with the well-established traditions of the baby shower and generalized excitement about the event among family and friends.

At the time of the birth, the Christian religion celebrates the new life with the rite of baptism. Judaism conducts a rite in which the infant is dedicated to God and named. Likewise, the Fellowship of Reason celebrates the birth of a child.

Transition from infancy to childhood

When a child is born, she is completely helpless. Her parents learn within weeks to identify her every peep and its meaning. Psychologists, it is claimed, have identified six different cries—pain, hunger, discomfort, fatigue, boredom, and tension discharge. The appropriate parental response is immediately forthcoming. In public, an infant is transported in a throne from marvelous place to marvelous place. Strangers present themselves before her to pay homage in hope of the bestowal of a smile. The infant learns from parental solicitude that the universe is oriented toward her own interests and responds to her every thought and desire. She is an adored queen served by gods. She is in paradise. The child's first knowledge is the existence of a loving, responsive, omnipotent, omniscient, and omnipresent Parent. The child's *concept* of Parent is precisely the concept of a being whom she may later in life, if raised under the influence of a religious mythology, identify as God.

The transition from infancy to childhood involves the child's realization that she is not the center of the universe, that there are no omnipotent, omniscient, and omnipresent gods, and that the physical laws of nature are not subject to the child's whims. In philosophical terms the maturing infant has to be changed from a subjectivist into an objectivist. In mythological-religious terms, like Adam and Eve in the biblical story, the child must eat of the tree of knowledge and be cast from the Garden of Eden.

It is the parents' responsibility acting as a proxy for reality to educate the child about the conditional nature of existence. The exercise of this responsibility is called parental discipline. The parent must start learning to say "no." Many parents have trouble converting to this stage. Children must learn the parental "no" in order to survive. At a later stage, adulthood, the parents must STOP acting as a proxy for reality and allow all of reality's consequences to flow.

For example, a child *will* learn not to touch the open flame of a gas stove by burning her hand in the flame. It is preferable, in order to avoid permanent physical damage or death, for the child to learn this lesson by the timely application of a parental "no." There are thousands of more or less extreme examples. Learning not to play in the street lest the child be run over is a more extreme example. Learning not to eat sweets between meals lest the child suffer malnutrition is a less extreme example.

Let us be clear—the parental "no" stands for the real world consequences of physical damage and death in case of error. The child *must* learn these real world consequences, if she is to survive. Parental discipline is one of the most loving acts a parent can perform.

At the Fellowship of Reason we recognize that parenting is the most important job in the world. There is no greater responsibility than the creation of a human being. A recognized expert in the field will teach a regular parenting course in the Fellowship of Reason.

Puberty:The teenage ritual

Puberty, the awakening of sexuality, is the most exciting and traumatic transition that we human beings undergo. In the English common law it was presumed to occur at age 12 for girls and at age 14 for boys. In the Fellowship of Reason we celebrate this event in a child's thirteenth year. Children attach significance to becoming "teenagers." The first teenage year is thir*teen*. Because of this numerical coincidence with the biological fact that human beings undergo puberty *around* the age of thirteen, it is appropriate to initiate our adolescents at or near their thirteenth birthdays.

Bas mitzvahs, bar mitzvahs, and confirmations mark the passage from childhood to adolescence. This crossing from the innocence of childhood to awareness of adult sexuality is one of the most difficult and ecstatic of human transitions. Adolescent mistakes during this time can impact the lives of many people. The specific mistake to which I refer is an unintended pregnancy. The victims of this mistake will be the child, the mother of the child, the father of the child, the mother's parents, and the father's parents. In a welfare state, taxpayers will also be victims.

It is objectively valuable to the adolescent undergoing the transformation to be informed about what she or he might expect. It is appropriate to celebrate this most profound of experiences. The adult celebrants are reminded of their own time of sexual awakening. The attention and celebration inform the adolescent that *something great* is about to happen. In accordance with our belief that parenting is the most important job in the world, the Fellowship of Reason regards the Teenage Ritual as one of the most important of our special rituals. We add an element of secrecy to augment the natural excitement and interest surrounding the Teenage Ritual. (See if you can divine the secret before it is revealed.)

Because sex education for adolescents is of universal concern to parents, the Fellowship of Reason will take advantage of the economic demand for adolescent sex education to market our Teenage Ritual to nonmembers. Not only will the Fellowship of Reason benefit from the public exposure arising as a consequence of the marketing efforts, but also we will certainly recruit new members from among our adolescent initiates, their parents, and siblings.

The most important element of the Teenage Ritual is a series of pre-initiation classes offered by various recognized experts in the fields of adolescent psychology, marriage counseling, and family planning.

Lessons 1 and 2: What Is Love?

At the first meeting, the children are informed that they are expected to learn one very specific lesson from the series of twelve one-hour classes. The children learn that they will be expected to bring a secret pass-phrase to graduation. They will not be told what the phrase is. They must discover it during the 12 hours of class. They must learn the phrase without parental assistance. The students are encouraged to discover the secret from the lessons and not to ask for adult assistance outside of class. They are free to discuss the matter among themselves. They are not permitted to ask older graduates of the Teenage Ritual for assistance. At graduation (which occurs during Celebration), upon presentation of the secret pass-phrase, the adolescent will be declared to be a responsible young adult and be given a significant token of her success.

The remainder of the first lesson is dedicated to the definition of values, the meaning of sacred (of the highest value), and the meaning of romantic love. A psychologist will talk about the different types of love, theories about why, biologically and evolutionarily, love exists, and the sometimes-overwhelming nature of the emotion. Examples from literature are cited such as Romeo and Juliet and Tristan and Iseult. For homework between lessons 1 and 2, the children are assigned to read Shakespeare's "Romeo and Juliet."

Lessons 3 and 4: Self-Sufficiency

The costs of living are explored in detail. Some children are assigned the task of calling apartment complexes in their vicinity to determine the rent and average utilities. Other children are asked to plan a month's worth of meals for a couple and to determine the cost by actually visiting a local grocery store. Another group will determine the monthly cost of transportation, including car payment, taxes, insurance, gas, oil, and maintenance. A final group of children is required to determine the monthly cost of an infant child, including formula, diapers, clothing, and daycare. The complete absence of employment opportunities for thirteen-year-olds is emphasized. As additional homework, the children are asked to carry a five-pound sack of sugar around for at least one hour per day between lessons. The sack of sugar represents an infant child's constant need for attention and care.

Lessons 5 and 6: Career Planning

The method by which a lifetime career is chosen is explored. The principle of "follow your bliss" is elaborated. The students are assigned, according to their interests, to determine the beginning yearly salaries for various occupations. Taxes as a necessary component of planning are discussed briefly.

Lessons 7 and 8: Sex, Birth Control, and STDs

Human sexuality is frankly explored, including the functioning of the sexual organs, intercourse, and the process of reproduction. All classes are coed. The students might experience embarrassment by the explicit discussion of this subject in a coed environment. The issue of embarrassment will be faced directly as an element of the class. The fact that human sexuality is a central fact of human nature and a central theme of human culture will be illustrated and explored. The legal prohibitions of various sexual activities are explained. For example, in some states the act of kissing an adolescent under age 16 is the crime of child molestation. Child molestation is a crime punishable by up to twenty years in prison if committed by an adult of age 17 or older. The reservation of the sexual act only to the most sacred of relationships is emphasized.

The methods of birth control are discussed and demonstrated. The legal availability of the various birth control products to adolescents is studied. The students are required to go to a pharmacy and determine the availability and cost of the various devices. Emphasis is placed upon the fact that the students are not yet ready for sex, even romantic kissing. Sexually transmitted diseases are discussed.

Lessons 9 and 10: What Is Marriage?

The legal institution of marriage is discussed. The sociological reasons for its existence are explored. The lifelong nature of the commitment is explored in detail, including the likely appearance during the marriage of other attractive people and how such encounters should be handled. The reservation of marriage to only fully matured and experienced adults is emphasized.

MARTIN L. COWEN III

Lesson 11: Parenting

The enormous subject of parenting is introduced. Parenting is the most important and most difficult job in the world. The question "Is bad parenting the root of all evil?" is explored.

Lesson 12: Conclusion

All of the lessons are related to the theme that sex is extremely important, that sexual activity has serious consequences for which the students will not be prepared for many years, and that birth control in the event of sex is crucially important until as husband and wife the couple make an informed and deliberate decision to become pregnant.

The students are given an index card on which to write the secret pass-phrase. They are instructed to write the secret pass-phrase on the card and to come next Sunday to Celebration for their initiation.

What is the secret pass-phrase? "Sex is sacred."

Marriage

The Fellowship of Reason recognizes marriage as one of the three most important commitments a person can make. (Children and career are the other two.) Premarital counseling for the couple is strongly encouraged, including an introduction to the subject of parenting. Being a part of a marital couple requires learned skills. A specialist can educate the couple and guide the couple to written sources for other crucial information.

The highly personal nature of the marriage relationship indicates that the parties determine the form of their celebration. The details of their vows are unique to each couple. An official authorized by local law to solemnize the marriage contract must perform the legal ceremony.

In the event a member of the Fellowship of Reason desires to celebrate her marriage among us, we are happy to participate. Certainly, the fact of a couple's marriage is noted and honored during Celebration.

Parenting

Parenting is the most important and most difficult job there is. Classes for married couples planning to have children are taught by recognized experts in the field. The question "Is bad parenting the root of all evil?" is explored.

Midlife changes

"Midway life's journey I was made aware that I had strayed into a dark forest, and the right path appeared not anywhere."—*Inferno* Dante

Professor of mythology Joseph Campbell tells the story of an aging friend who says that you know you are getting old when, having climbed to the top of a ladder you placed to clean the gutters of your home, you find that you have placed your ladder against the wrong wall. In the same way, after years of working at a career and finally reaching the top rung of the ladder of success, some people find that they have placed their ladders against the wrong wall. They find that what they have worked for is not, after all, so valuable. After twenty years in sales, having achieved all the highest awards and having lived the good life of spend, spend, spend, you may find that you wish you had spent those twenty years pursuing your childhood interest in sculpture. You had been afraid to follow the path of art because it was uncertain and unlikely to be financially rewarding. Instead you chose the safe, well-worn path of sales. (Sales need not be a well-worn path and for many it is the right path. This is merely an example.) At such times a crisis ensues, the so-called midlife crisis.

This crisis is a dangerous time, because the person in crisis can make foolish decisions in a panic to extricate himself from the crisis. Counseling is strongly encouraged.

Parents can also experience a midlife crisis when their children grow up. A couple who has dedicated their lives to the raising of their family need to plan for a life after the children finally leave home.

The Fellowship of Reason addresses these transition times. In chapter 4 I showed how to plan well in advance to avoid these pitfalls. But even the best-laid plans sometimes go astray and for that eventuality the Fellowship of Reason has a backup.

The "Look-Up" ritual occurs during Celebration and takes place annually January. The New Year is a traditional time for self-evaluation. Volunteer members are called upon to read aloud the written purpose of their lives. This public statement calls upon the performer and the congregation to reflect upon the importance of pursuing meaningful goals.

Death

Funerals are for the living. In the Fellowship of Reason we take considerable pains to celebrate the life of recently departed loved ones. The bereaved needs an adequate time to suffer his loss. The funeral is just the beginning of that process.

LESSER RITUALS

Bless you

The expression "God bless you" means "I love you and wish you the best." It expresses a real emotion that can and should be expressed. However, among members of our moral community the reference to God can be confusing. For members of the Fellowship of Reason then, a modification of this important expression is in order. Since our highest value is ourselves, the expression becomes simply "bless you."

Incidentally, "good bye" derives from "God bless you."

Reflections prior to dining

Religious people often ask that someone "say a blessing" before eating. Members of the Fellowship of Reason often enjoy the ritual of the blessing.

Consider the context when you sit down to a formal dinner. Someone has purchased the ingredients for the meal. Someone has prepared the meal, often with great attention to nutrition, flavor, aroma, and visual appeal. Someone has provided a safe and attractive environment in which to enjoy the meal. Someone has provided a table setting of fine china, silver, and crystal upon which to enjoy the feast. Family and friends have gathered with you to dine. The meal is nourishment for your body. The fellowship of the event is nourishment for your soul. The art of the meal and the setting are a joy to behold. The dinner serves your precious life and the lives of your dinner companions.

After serving the meal and before beginning to enjoy, it is rational to acknowledge the meaning of this important occasion.

A toastmaster should draw everyone's attention and say a few appropriate words. These words might be a poem, an old saying, or some brief remarks especially written for the event. Eye contact is appropriate and, depending upon the tastes and relationship of the celebrants, holding hands around the table.

The following consecration is illustrative of the tone appropriate for an important family reunion.

"What a great occasion! We are gathered here together in the safety of our home, each of us taking a moment from our busy, separate lives, to enjoy this wonderful meal with ones we love. Let this evening be a special time in our lives, a blessed stopping point in which we can simply enjoy who we are, where we are, and what we are doing. Let us enjoy this magnificent *now* with family and friends. Thank you, mother, for preparing this beautiful meal."

For a regular family meal O.T. Nelson suggests this little saying: "As we have earned this food, so must we earn all that is valuable in our lives (Nelson 1977, p. 173)."

We must be mindful of the times of our lives. It is up to each of us to create meaningful, personal traditions to honor our families, our friends, and ourselves.

Reflections upon retiring for the evening

As we discussed in chapter 1, personal reflection is an important tool for appreciating your precious life. It is difficult to find time to do this seemingly unproductive activity in our busy days. One problem is unrealistic expectations. If you expect great insights each time you set aside ten minutes for reflection, you will be disappointed. At the end of the day just before bed is a good time for personal reflection and meditation. Two good questions to consider are these: What is good about my life? And, what are my life's purposes and what do I need to do about them tomorrow?

Of course, this is *personal* reflection and so the questions upon which you choose to reflect are up to you. Sometimes you may not have the mental energy to even think about these questions. In such a case, do not think. Simply sit and empty your mind of all thought. The point of this activity is to *allow* yourself time to appreciate your life even if you fail to do it on a particular occasion. In addition, not thinking allows issues pushed to the back of your consciousness by the press of ordinary day-to-day business to rise to the level of consciousness so that you might become aware of them.

If you do choose to consider what is good about your life, look to your intimate relationships, your friends, your work, your health, and your political and economic freedom. When considering your life's purposes, look to your marriage, your children, and your work. Be sure to think about specific issues that you need to address tomorrow before retiring. Put that magnificent fact of existence, your mind, to work upon your problem. By calling the problem to mind just before bed, you are programming your unconscious thought processes to solve the problem while you sleep.

This activity is not an attempt to influence a divine being or any form of magic. This activity is *routine* thoughtfulness. It is rational to be thoughtful.

Anniversaries, birthdays, and graduations

Whenever important days such as anniversaries, birthdays, and graduations are known, specific attention is called to those enjoying these events during Celebration.

Winter solstice/Christmas

While most of the rest of the world celebrates the religious holidays of Christmas and Hanukkah, members of the Fellowship of Reason celebrate the lengthening days following the winter solstice among friends and family with the exchange of gifts and good wishes. Our winter solstice celebrations honor the virtues of benevolence and generosity.

Vernal equinox/Easter

The religious holiday of Easter celebrates the "supreme ordeal" in Christian mythology. I describe this mythological element and Easter in the next chapter. The Fellowship of Reason does not celebrate Easter as such. We do not believe that man has Original Sin for which some atonement must be made. We do, however, enjoy and celebrate springtime.

FELLOWSHIP OF REASON

Independence Day

The Fellowship of Reason recognizes that the creation of America by our Founding Fathers has made possible the unprecedented freedom and prosperity that we enjoy today. We are full participants in the American celebration of Independence Day.

Thanksgiving

As a day of rest to celebrate our achievements, we at the Fellowship of Reason enjoy Thanksgiving. We offer thanks to ourselves as achievers of value and to those achievers that have contributed to our success today and in the past.

Oaths

"Do you solemnly affirm that you will tell the truth, the whole truth, and nothing but the truth." Civil oaths are useful and appropriate to call a person's attention to the importance of the occasion of the party's testimony and to the legal consequences of perjury.

CONCLUSION

Some rational individualists are afraid of rituals and for good reason. Historically, many rituals have been evil things, often involving human sacrifice, literal or figurative. Even the Eucharist, the religious sacrament of Holy Communion, is symbolic ritual cannibalism. We of the Fellowship of Reason reject the destruction of sacred earthly values for the sake of a mythological afterlife. We reject irrationalism in any form. The Fellowship of Reason hereby reclaims rational ritual for the purpose of celebrating human life on earth and reinforcing life-sustaining principles.

In the next chapter we will learn who is our Jesus/ Buddha/Moses and what is our mythology.

Chapter 11 — Mythology

The hero's will is not that of his ancestors or of his society, but his own. This will to be oneself is heroism.
—Ortega y Gasset 2000, pp. 148–149

The sacred books of Judaism, Christianity, Islam, Buddhism, and the Veda are the best repositories of the ideas that mattered most to our ancestors, and to ignore them is an act of childish conceit. But it is equally naïve to believe that whatever was written down in the past contains an absolute truth that lasts forever. —Csikszentmihalyi 1997, p. 3

The beauty of the Hero's Journey model is that it not only describes a pattern in myths and fairytales, but it's also an accurate map of the territory one must travel to become... a human being. —Vogler 1992, p. 281

Ultimately, fully evolved heroes feel compassion for their apparent enemies and transcend rather than destroy them.
—Vogler 1992, p. 65

"Hey, Martin, you seem to have created a new religion here.

...Who is your Jesus?"

Heroes

Religion and philosophy have a common purpose—to teach us how to live. Religion, though, is a primitive form of philosophy based upon faith. Philosophy is based upon reason. This book describes not a new religion, but a new philosophy, or, more accurately, a new synthesis of philosophy, psychology, and mythology. The synthesis is based upon the work of many philosophers, including Aristotle, David Kelley, Pierre Hadot, David L. Norton, and Ayn Rand. Among the influential psychologists are Nathaniel Branden, Mihali Csikszentmihalyi, Victor Frankl, Carl G. Jung, and Abraham Maslow. The ideas of mythologist Joseph Campbell and storyteller Christopher Vogler are discussed in this chapter.

Most religions have a mythical or historical hero. For Buddhism, he is the Buddha. For Christianity, he is Jesus. For Judaism, he is Moses or Abraham or David. For Islam, he is Mohammed. The ancient Greeks worshipped Zeus and his entourage. The ancient Romans had Jupiter and the rest. All of these heroes have one thing in common—they are all human beings or human beings writ large.

Human beings anthropomorphize their gods for a reason. Religion's purpose is to teach human beings how to live, not like gods, but like human beings. Religious heroes are the role models for the faithful. *Human* beings require *human* role models. Christians aspire to be like Jesus. Buddhists aspire to be like Buddha. Muslims aspire to be like Mohammed. Jews aspire to be like Moses.

In his book *The Hero with a Thousand Faces*, Joseph Campbell demonstrates that all mythological heroes are manifestations of the hero archetype—a standard mythological hero figure. There are, it appears, thousands of heroes to admire. Because the human race is chock full of heroes, the Fellowship of Reason does not have *a* hero, but many heroes. Our heroes are real men and women without supernatural powers who were, are, and will be.

THE FUNCTIONS OF MYTHOLOGY

Mythology has served humankind for millennia. Thanks to mythologist Joseph Campbell, we now have a comprehensive view of how it has done so. We have a greater understanding of the functions of mythology. Because we understand more fully the *subject* of mythology, we need no longer be bound to a particular state-sponsored or religion-sponsored mythology. Heresy is no longer a crime. Witches are not burned. Heretics are not tortured to death. Dissent is welcome, not merely tolerated. Dissent is valuable because it demands that one's assertions be constantly tested, validated, and proved. Reason is our guide, not uncritical adherence to ancient myths and dogmas.

Joseph Campbell divides the functions of mythology into four categories: mystical, cosmological, sociological, and pedagogical.

Mystical

"Mysteries are not necessarily miracles," said Goethe. Only a fool would claim that humankind has discovered even a small percentage of what there is to learn about man and the universe. There will always be mysteries for human beings to solve. For each individual, the most personally important mystery of them all is "how am I to live and be happy?" Mythology serves the function of reminding us of the mystery.

The place where human beings live, all of existence, is a sacred place, not apart from, but because of the presence of human beings. Evoking awe, humility, respect, and reverence for existence as such, the place where humankind lives, is an important function of mythology.

Cosmological

Another historical function of mythology has been to explain from whence the world and human beings come. This function is now overtaken by science. The answer is still a mystery. The question will certainly engage astronomers, biologists, geologists, and physicists for thousands of years to come.

Sociological

The third function of mythology is to illustrate and justify the individual's place in society. Our current myths as reflected in popular movies and stories illustrate the dominance of individualism. That is, of course, good news for rational individualists.

Pedagogical

The fourth function of mythology is to teach human beings how to live and be happy. To this function I would like to attend more fully by discussing some elements of the Hero's Journey.

The Hero's Journey

Thanks to the work of Joseph Campbell the Fellowship of Reason can draw moral lessons from all of mythology. We now recognize the main functions of mythology and one important pattern that recurs in many myths.

Myths tell stories that give human beings insight on how they should live. Human life consists of goal-directed action. The ultimate but abstract goal is life—health and happiness. Health and happiness are the physical and mental manifestations of a successful human life. There are countless intermediate, concrete goals. A human life can be understood as thousands of separate goal-directed activities, some in series, some occurring simultaneously. This may be a simple task—I find I am out of eggs, so I go to the store, buy some eggs, and return home—or a complex one—I find that I am lonely for community, but that the traditional religious experience is not meaningful. So I write a book, create the Fellowship of Reason, and go to Celebration every Sunday.

The pattern in mythology identified by Joseph Campbell is called the Hero's Journey. This pattern is actually the pattern of all goal-directed human action. Understanding this pattern in myths and stories provides us with invaluable information about how we can successfully live our lives. Knowing where we are during our own adventures provides us with important information that allows us to proceed with greater confidence and improves our chances of ultimate success.

The stages of the hero's journey are the ordinary world, the call to adventure, refusing the call, crossing the first threshold, meeting the mentor, accepting tests and challenges, meeting allies and enemies, approaching the inmost cave, enduring the supreme ordeal, seizing the reward, traveling the road back, resurrection, and returning with the elixir. Among the hero's companions are the herald, the mentor, threshold guardians, the trickster, shapeshifters, allies, enemies, and the shadow. We will discuss some of these stages and companions.

Ordinary world

Most stories establish the hero in her ordinary world before the adventure begins. A common adventure involves the hero seeking justice following a crime committed against the hero's family. Such a story might begin by showing the hero at home and happy among her loving family. After the hero's ordinary world is established, the call to adventure might be heralded by the family dog barking excitedly at the approach of the criminals who will wipe out the hero's family. The ordinary world need not be established at the beginning of the story. Sometimes, for dramatic purposes, the story begins with the call to adventure or at some other point in the story, perhaps at the supreme ordeal. In real life we can imagine being called to a new adventure and we can compare our present life (the ordinary world) to the imagined life of the adventure (the special world of the adventure). For example, a young person who has not yet decided to have children can appreciate her present lifestyle free of parental obligations. Without children, she can travel, dine out, and go to parties. The adventure of parenthood will involve a dramatic change in her freedom to do the things as a single person she takes for granted. The mental exercise of projecting lifestyle changes occasioned by a new adventure is very useful in deciding whether or not to embark on that new adventure, especially big adventures like starting a career, getting married, or becoming a parent.

Call to adventure

The call to adventure in stories is some kind of change in the ordinary world of the hero. The hero's family is wiped out by invading barbarians. A dead body is discovered in a library mysteriously locked from the inside with a puddle of water beside the body. The detective hero is called to investigate the mystery. In real life, all of us are constantly called to new adventures. A hero sees a beautiful girl and thinks he is in love. The hero is called to the adventure of romance. A hero is fired from her job. The hero is called to the adventure of finding new employment. Our hero decides to have a baby. Now there is an adventure! Or you are out of eggs. Adventures range from the banal to the sublime.

Any call to action in your life can be understood as a call to adventure. So understood, you may anticipate that you will be thrust into the Hero's Journey, including all of its elements.

You are not required to heed every call to adventure. In fact, you cannot, because life is too short. But sometimes refusing the call to adventure is costly.

Refusing the call

Often in actual life, and not infrequently in myths and popular tales, we encounter the dull case of the call unanswered; for it is always possible to turn the ear to other interests. Refusal of the summons converts the adventure into its negative. Walled in boredom, hard work, or 'culture,' the subject loses the power of significant affirmative action and becomes a victim to be saved. His flowering world becomes a wasteland of dry stones and his life feels meaningless (Campbell 1972, p. 59).

Many chronic human problems can be grouped under the category "refusal of the call to adventure." I would like to point out a few.

Adolescence

Perhaps the greatest biological call to adventure is the call to the adventure of sexual maturity. When a child enters adolescence, hormones pour into her bloodstream causing huge changes in her body and emotions. These changes practically force the adventure of sexuality upon the child. A friend told me about her birth as a sexual being. At age thirteen our hero was psychologically a little girl who played with dolls. She was invited by a friend to go to Florida. While our hero was in Florida she found that boys were interested in her. She flirted for the first time. Our hero was fascinated by the attention of boys. When she returned to Atlanta she literally put her dolls away and never played with them again. Her acceptance of the call to the adventure of sexual maturity happened over a weekend.

The call to the adventure of sexual maturity can be refused or delayed. There are ancient myths that explore the consequences of the refusal of the call to sexual maturity.

The French film *La Belle et La Bête* (1946) is a story about a young girl's refusal of the call to sexual maturity. In this fairytale a young man loves Beauty but she refuses his advances because, she thinks, she must stay with her father. She is a daddy's girl. Of course, this will not do in myth or in real life. If Beauty is to live her life fully she must give up her life as a child and accept her life as a wife and mother. That is the way of things. Because Beauty refuses her lover and her proper life as an adult woman, wife, and mother, she throws everyone into the negative of the adventure (in Joseph Campbell's terms). People are going to suffer and die because of Beauty's refusal of the call to the adventure of sexual maturity. The antagonists are Belle's father and the raging passion of her young, would-be lover. The Beast represents this raging passion. The Beast captures the father and will kill him unless the father sends the Beast one of his daughters. Belle is sent. While physically Belle is with her lover, spiritually she is not—yet. She experiences trials and challenges as the prisoner of the Beast, but finally she chooses sexual maturity over being a daddy's girl. Significantly, Diana, the goddess of fertility, kills the frustrated would-be lover. The Beast dies and turns into a man who looks exactly like the formerly frustrated would-be lover. While in the literal story the young man is killed, the spiritual meaning is that the existence of the "frustrated" would-be lover ends, as does the existence of the unsatisfied raging passion represented by the Beast. Both are born again into a new, single being, the satisfied lover of Beauty. The father survives too by passing into his proper role as father of the bride.

Half-way Decisions

A common failing is to want to have one's cake and to eat it too. This failing can be seen as a refusal of the call to adventure.

I used to own a sailboat. I decided, half-heartedly, to sell the boat. I wanted to sell the boat and I wanted to keep it. So I listed the boat with a broker who had no experience with this particular type of boat. After months of inactivity I cancelled his contract. I learned by doing some minimal research that I had overpriced the boat. I tried to sell the boat myself for almost two more years. All of these efforts to sell the boat were half-hearted. I was not fully committed to selling the boat that I had loved.

I had one foot in the adventure of selling the boat and one foot out.

FELLOWSHIP OF REASON

Finally, I took the boat to an international marketplace for boats and placed the boat with a broker who specialized in this particular type of boat. I followed the broker's suggestions. I was fully committed to selling the boat. I was using a professional boat broker in the largest boat market in the world. In less than 90 days I achieved the goal of my adventure—I sold the boat.

Thinking mythologically, I know that my failure was in refusing to fully accept the call to adventure.

I suggested in recounting Beauty's story that the refusal of the call is the way of death. How, you may ask, is my failure to fully embrace the adventure of selling the boat the way of death? Well, the boat costs about $1,500 per month to own. I had been trying, half-heartedly, to sell the boat for 34 months. I lost $51,000 due to my lack of full participation in this adventure. The loss of $51,000, while not fully death, is certainly the loss of value.

Full Acceptance—Gattaca

Let me contrast the refusal of the call to adventure with a full acceptance of the call to adventure illustrated in the movie *Gattaca*. The subtitle of this film is "There is no gene for the human spirit." The hero of this movie is a "love child," not born out of wedlock, but born outside of genetic control. In the near future world of *Gattaca* the complete control of the genetic makeup of children is possible. It is also preferred. Even though it is illegal, society discriminates based upon the quality of a person's genetic makeup. Our hero wants to be an astronaut, but, because of his genetic makeup, he will not be accepted through normal channels. However, our hero will not be stopped. He decides to get a partner, a genetically perfect paraplegic. He uses his partner's bodily substances (blood, urine, skin, and hair) containing perfect genetic material to fool the authorities as to his own imperfect genetic makeup. Our hero stops at nothing to achieve his goal. He works as a janitor. He studies and exercises tirelessly. He agrees to have three inches of bone added to his legs so that he will be taller. He achieves his goal.

One side plot of the movie reveals his secret of success. Our hero has a genetically perfect brother. Our hero has never beaten his perfect brother

163

at anything. One day they decide to race straight out into the ocean. Our hero wins, to the shock of his brother. At the end of the movie the hero explains the secret of his success to his perfect brother. "I didn't save anything for the trip back." In other words, our hero was prepared to drown in the ocean in order to swim farther than his brother. Our hero was nothing but his goal. Nothing, not even his own life, stood in the way of the achievement of his goal. This is the full acceptance of the call to adventure. When you are able to say, "There is no turning back. I will succeed or cease to exist. My success is my existence."

The Completion of an Adventure

In life many things come to an end. When the end comes, there is a new call to adventure—the adventure of living without whatever it was that came to an end.

At some point in everyone's life, if he is lucky, he will complete his life's work, his magnum opus. There is an old story about the youthful prodigy, who, following some great achievement early in life, spends fruitless future years trying to recapture faded glory. When a person finishes a great adventure, she must be prepared to live on without the adventure that has recently ended. She must find a new personal destiny.

When a child reaches maturity and goes out into the world, the parent's job is done. A parent who fails to recognize the end of the adventure of parenthood may find herself seriously depressed. This is a very common problem. A person who is aware of the Hero's Journey will be prepared for the call to adventure that the completion of a great adventure represents. She will have a great new adventure lined up.

Loss of Relationship

Most people experience the end of a romantic relationship at some time in their lives. Most people have at some time or other been "dumped." A response to being "dumped" is to hate the dumper. Another response is to accept the fact that tastes differ and just because an individual thinks himself the ultimate romantic conquest another need not share that view. The breech of solemn promises may, of course, justify righteous indignation. The end of a romance is a call to adventure—the adventure of living a life without the lost love.

Accidental Loss

Some adventures are necessitated by accidents. For example, the actor who played Superman, Christopher Reeve, broke his neck in a riding accident. He was for a long time depressed and not sure he wanted to live. After a time and with his wife's assurance that "you're still you" he was able to accept his call to adventure to live his life as a quadriplegic. He is now widely regarded as an American hero. Reeve defines a hero in his book *Still Me* (1999) as "an ordinary individual who finds the strength to persevere and endure in spite of overwhelming obstacles."

A person who gives up in the face of such a tragedy might turn to drugs, or evil, or even suicide.

An example of the refusal of the call to live life as a disabled person is offered by the novel *Moby-Dick* by Hermann Melville. Ahab lost his leg to the great white whale—certainly a tragic accident. Unlike Christopher Reeve, though, Ahab could not accept the loss of his leg. He determined to exact revenge from the dumb animal that maimed him. Here is an entire story based upon the refusal of the call to adventure.

Hear Ahab's words:

> Toward thee I roll, thou all-destroying but unconquering whale; to the last I grapple with thee; from hell's heart I stab at thee; for hate's sake I spit my last breath at thee. Sink all coffins and all hearses to one common pool! and since neither can be mine, let me then tow to pieces, while still chasing thee, though tied to thee, thou damned whale!

The refusal of the call to adventure is the way of death.

Full Acceptance of Santiago

Another great mythological example of the full acceptance of the call to adventure is Ernest Hemingway's *The Old Man and the Sea*. The parallels between this story and *Moby-Dick* are very interesting. Both stories are about a man trying to catch a sea creature with unfailing resolve, yet one story is negative and the other positive.

The Old Man and the Sea represents the idea that "In great attempts, it is glorious even to fail."

The comparison of these two stories also shows that it is not always easy to know when you are refusing a call to adventure. You cannot do everything and certainly every possible adventure need not be pursued. But there is a clue to which adventures should be pursued in the comparison of these two great stories.

We can see from the following quotation that Santiago was as determined to get his fish as Ahab was to get his whale.

"Fish," he said softly, aloud, "I'll stay with you until I am dead."

He'll stay with me too, I suppose, the old man thought and he waited for it to be light. It was cold now in the time before daylight and he pushed against the wood to be warm. I can do it as long as he can, he thought.

For Santiago there was no turning back. He was saving nothing for the return trip.

The difference between Santiago and Ahab is their motivation for action. Santiago is driven by his love for his own identity and personal excellence. He is a fisherman. Ahab is driven by his hatred of his own identity. Ahab is a one-legged man. Ahab turned his refusal to accept the loss of his leg into hatred for a senseless beast. Love versus hate is an old theme. The lesson is, again in Joseph Campbell's terms, to follow your bliss, follow your love, not your hate.

As proof of Santiago's intention I offer this short quotation. Santiago has been struggling for a long time with the fish and Santiago is hungry. "I wish I could feed the fish, he thought. He is my brother. But I must kill him and keep strong to do it." And a little later: "Then he was sorry for the great fish that had nothing to eat and his determination to kill him never relaxed in his sorrow for him. How many people will he feed, he thought. But are they worthy to eat him? No, of course not. There is no one worthy to eat him from the manner of his behavior and his great dignity."

Crossing the first threshold

The stage in which the hero moves from the ordinary world into the special world of the adventure is called the crossing of the first threshold. In the novel *Cold Mountain: A Novel* (Frazier 1998) the hero steps out of the window of a Civil War hospital, becomes a deserter, and begins his journey home to the mountains of North Carolina. He literally crosses the threshold of the window to begin his adventure.

More interesting in real life than the crossing of the threshold to adventure are the emotions and people you meet at the first threshold—the threshold guardians. These are numerous and most interesting. If there is only one thing you learn from mythology, learn about your threshold guardians.

Threshold guardians are any characters and circumstances in a story that try to stop the hero from going on his adventure. In *Star Wars* Luke Skywalker's aunt and uncle are his threshold guardians. They want Luke to spend one more year on the farm before going off to school. They sure do not want Luke going off with the Jedi Knight Obi-Wan Kanobi. The Empire overcomes Luke's threshold guardians by killing them, supplying Luke with an additional impetus for his adventure—revenge.

In real life your threshold guardians are all those reasons you can think of for not doing what you ought to do. The beauty of identifying your excuses as threshold guardians is that you know immediately from mythology that threshold guardians *must* be defeated or circumvented. Rather than cowering in fear the rest of your life, you will have the courage to find ways to get past your threshold guardians.

Fear of Rejection or Failure

Fear of rejection or failure is everyone's number one threshold guardian. Nowhere is this threshold guardian more active than in romantic adventures. Everyone knows that having an intimate relationship is important for life and happiness. Achieving an intimate relationship is not an adventure than can safely be avoided, if one is to live and be happy. Identifying romance as a *mandatory* adventure in life is immensely helpful. Identifying one's fear of rejection as a threshold guardian is, likewise, immensely helpful. Having made those identifications, you can draw from thousands of other successful mythic adventures the reassuring knowledge that the romantic adventure is a well-known path. Billions of people have been, are, and will be on that path. There are many techniques for surviving and succeeding in this adventure. You will have the knowledge that, not only *must* you go on the adventure, you are very likely to succeed.

In real life and in mythology, threshold guardians often cannot be defeated in a head-on battle. The threshold guardian "fear of rejection" must be embraced and accepted. Failure *is* a possible outcome in all adventures.

Your Parents

The hopes and dreams of one's parents constitute another real-life threshold guardian. As a child, a person ought to obey his parents. A mature adult is autonomous, self-knowledgeable, self-responsible, and self-fulfilling. Parents are, or should be, out of the picture, except as interested, respected, and trusted advisors. Yet some adults remain in their role as obedient children, failing to move fully into the adventure of mature adulthood. Mature adulthood is another *mandatory* adventure if one is to live and be happy.

This threshold guardian, the opinion of your parents, belongs to a general class of threshold guardians called "others." The opinions of others, generally, are to be considered and evaluated. If you find the opinion valid, follow it. If not, courteously decline to follow the advice of others and live by your own best judgment.

Self-Imposed Expectations

I know a man who at age fifty lives with his parents. He has no job, though he is intelligent, benevolent, and able-bodied. He, occasionally, has a job interview. The reason he does not work is that he sees himself as an oceanographer and he will take no other job. There are no such jobs where he lives. My friend's view of himself as an oceanographer is a formidable threshold guardian. His failure to move past this guardian is costing my friend his self-esteem. He sees himself as incapable and unworthy of life. That appraisal is true so long as he remains paralyzed before his own self-imposed and unreasonable expectations. The adventure of being a productive person is another *mandatory* adventure.

How is my friend, the would-be oceanographer, to get past his threshold guardian? I hope he will read this book.

Crippling Pain

Pat Conroy's novel *Prince of Tides* (1986) dramatizes the consequences of refusing to live through the emotional consequences of a traumatic event. The hero, Tom Wingo, and his twin sister Savannah are dysfunctional adults. Savannah is suicidal. Tom is depressed, unemployed, and a miserable husband. Both are blocked from living healthy lives by their failure to deal with painful emotions caused by a repressed childhood trauma. They cannot get on with the adventure of their lives. The crippling pain is a threshold guardian to the rest of their lives.

Popular action films often contain damaged characters of this sort. The *Lethal Weapon* movies focus on the relationship between a burned-out cop whose wife has been killed and a psychologically healthy cop who is happily married with children. The burned-out cop is on the verge of suicide as the story begins.

The threshold guardian is defeated by being embraced, accepted, and incorporated into the hero. In other words, the excruciating emotional pain of dealing with the loss is accepted and fully experienced.

Finding a mentor

Most stories involve some type of personal growth for the hero. The same is true in real life. Healthy human beings grow through the whole of their lives. Heroes often grow as a result of contact with some type of teacher. The people a mythological hero learns from are called mentors. King Arthur's Merlin is the quintessential mentor. Mentors in myth and in real life can be found everywhere and it is crucial to be aware of this. Any of the hero's companions—the herald, the mentor, threshold guardians, the trickster, shapeshifters, allies, enemies, or the shadow—can serve as a mentor.

Once I gave a talk about the Hero's Journey. A member of the audience asked a difficult question. I initially reacted (in my thoughts) badly to the questioner. However, upon reflection, I noticed a weakness in my talk and discovered a powerful solution. Rather than being an "enemy," this questioner turned out to be a "mentor." I sent an e-mail thanking him.

Enduring the supreme ordeal

Many stories include a scene in which the hero, it seems, has failed in his adventure. In fact, the hero may even be on the verge of death. Suddenly, his fortunes reverse and the hero survives, often to complete his adventure. In James Bond stories this is the moment when the megalomaniac has Bond in his clutches and plans to kill Bond in some spectacular fashion. Invariably, Bond escapes to defeat the evil one and save the world.

In the mythology of Christianity, the supreme ordeal is celebrated every Easter. Jesus Christ is betrayed by his Apostles, tried, condemned to death, and crucified. All seems lost. On the third day following his crucifixion he rises miraculously from the dead. Jesus ascends into heaven victorious, even over death. The sins of mankind are forgiven. Easter is scheduled on the first Sunday following the first full moon following the spring equinox. The sun "returns" from the Southern Hemisphere at the spring equinox. The moon is in its glory when full. The first Sunday following these two important celestial events is appropriately chosen for Easter. The celestial sequence of the disappearance of the last sliver of the waning moon, the one night of no moon, and the return on the "third day" of the first sliver of the new moon, corresponds to the timing of the Easter event. Jesus dies on Good Friday, is dead on Saturday, and rises from the dead on Easter Sunday. The egg, a symbol of new life, is an icon of Easter.

The celebration of the supreme ordeal in myths and stories is very important psychologically. Many of the goal-directed activities of human life are difficult. The hero may achieve many goals only with the last ounce of effort. Even when the hero herself thinks she is lost, she must not give up. Victory may be at hand.

Persistence is an important virtue. If individuals gave up when their adventures became difficult, very little in life would be accomplished. This is the lesson of the supreme ordeal.

Film critics and other social commentators sometimes whine about the preference of American audiences for happy endings. I believe most people, especially action-oriented people, need happy endings. We see films for a purpose. In our own lives, we are in the middle of many adventures. The most important adventures of our lives—career, marriage, and parenthood—involve decades of effort. The results of our efforts are not immediate. We—the members of the audience—need to see that success, even though off in the uncertain future, is possible. The happy ending serves this purpose.

Returning with the elixir

When the goal of the adventure is achieved, the hero often returns to his ordinary world. More often than not he is changed for the better as a result of his adventure. Sometimes the hero does not survive his adventure. In that case it is often the audience that returns to their homes with the elixir—whatever the lesson of the story was.

Many stories simply end when the hero returns with the reward. However, some stories illustrate the very common problem of the ordinary world's reluctance to accept the returning hero and his boon.

Any creative person or entrepreneur experiences the difficulty of selling his creation or idea to other people. Mythologically speaking, any creation or idea is itself the result of a hero's successful return from an adventure with his elixir or reward or boon. Stories sometimes illustrate the problems heroes have upon returning to the ordinary world with the elixir. In Ayn Rand's *Atlas Shrugged* (1957) Hank Rearden created Rearden Metal, a science-fictional metal with marvelous properties. His "hero's journey" to create the metal is only alluded to in the novel. His Herculean efforts to sell the product to a skeptical public are more fully depicted. In the movie version of Carl Sagan's book *Contact* (1997) Jodie Foster's character goes on a fantastic voyage into the cosmos. Upon her return, she would like to share with the people of her ordinary world the beauty and love she discovered on her fantastic adventure. Sadly, though, she is hauled before a congressional committee to defend herself against charges of participation in a huge fraud. In the 1951 film *The Man in the White Suit* Alex Guinness' character is a brilliant scientist on the trail of the discovery of an indestructible thread. He apparently makes his discovery and attempts to bring it to the world. The owners of the mills, the workers in the mills, and even the poor old wash woman are united in their efforts to stop the introduction of the scientist's great discovery to the market. The hero is saved from murder by the unexpected failure of his thread. The story ends with the scientist, suddenly enthused with a new insight into his scientific problem, marching confidently off.

Conclusion

Every good story has something to teach us; otherwise it would not be written or preserved. I cannot hope to cover all that mythology has to teach us about being human and achieving happiness in one chapter or even in a whole book. My intention is merely to give a taste of the value to be found in myths and stories and to answer the question, "Who is our Jesus?"

We enjoy myths and stories because they provide information and examples that we can apply to living our own lives successfully. Knowing about the Hero's Journey, the common pattern of mythology discovered by Joseph Campbell, enables us to apply, in a more rigorous and structured way, the knowledge imparted by myths and stories.

The Fellowship of Reason is not bound to any particular state-sponsored or religion-sponsored mythology. We look forward to learning all that mythology has to teach.

In the last chapter we will learn compelling reasons to start a Fellowship of Reason in your community.

Chapter 12—What's In It for Me?

It is my thought, that the wealth and glory of the Western world, and of the modern world as well (in so far as it is still in spirit Western), is a function of this respect for the individual.
—Campbell 1990, p. 222

[T]he reader's intimation of his own unique, irreplaceable, potential worth ... is entitled to cultural sponsorship by means of institutions designed to afford it nurture and guidance.
—Norton 1976, pp. 355–356

[T]he meaningful living that is conditioned upon self-truth and self-responsibility will seldom occur in the world until it receives nurture in its earliest intimations by supportive cultural institutions. —Norton 1976, p. xi

The form in which religions have presented their truths—myths, revelations, holy texts—no longer compels belief in an era of scientific rationality, even though the substance of the truths may have remained unchanged. A vital new religion may one day arise again. In the meantime, those who seek consolation in existing churches often pay for their peace of mind with a tacit agreement to ignore a great deal of what is known about the way the world works.—Csikszentmihalyi 1991, p. 14

The community today is the planet, not the bounded nation.
—Campbell 1972, p. 388

In this final chapter I would like to give you several reasons for creating or joining a Fellowship of Reason in your community.

SACRED BEING

Have you ever been in love? Have you ever isolated your capacity for that emotion and looked at it? Have you put aside the desperation, the desire, the need, the ache for your beloved and just *marveled* at your capacity to feel that way? That is your capacity to experience the sacred.

Romantic love is a sacred emotion. Love for your children is a sacred emotion. Love for one's capacity as an artist is a sacred emotion. Love for your own life is a sacred emotion. But these things, a beloved, children, your creative capacity, your life, must be achieved and they require work. The Fellowship of Reason will help you in that work.

The goal of your life should be to build and arrange your existence so that every moment of your life you are where you want to be and doing what you want to do. The goal of all human beings should be to arrange their lives in such a way that only sacred actions and objects occupy the precious time of their lives. Such is the state I call "sacred being." Spirituality is the art of sacred being.

NOW MOMENTS

When I was 18 years old I traveled with my college chorus to New York City to sing on the stage of Carnegie Hall. We stayed in the Wellington Hotel on Seventh Avenue around the corner from the concert hall. I went into the small bar adjacent to the hotel lobby and sat at a small round table bearing a white tablecloth under a tiny white spotlight. I ordered my first martini. The perfectly clear gin was served "up" (no ice, but chilled) in an elegant glass with a twist of lemon. I remember sitting there in the dark room just looking at my drink on the white cloth under the light. I felt so grown up.

That was a "now moment." A now moment is an occasion when you are not going anywhere. You have arrived. You are content and captured by the pleasure of the moment. I say captured because so often, wherever we are and whatever we are doing, we are not fully "in" the moment. Instead we are worrying about the past or planning for the future. In a now moment, both the past and future are out of mind. You live fully in the present.

Listening to music can be the occasion of a now moment. Golfers experience now moments on the links. Sun worshipers on Mallory Dock in Key West experience a now moment watching the sun set into the sea. Generally, the enjoyment of art, friends, sports, fine dining, natural beauty, and romance can occasion now moments.

One of the secrets of successful churches is the creation of now moments for the members.

Since this secret has been revealed, perhaps you can help us to create such moments during Celebration by leaving behind your worries, temporarily forgetting about the future, and experiencing the pleasure of this moment in your life among friends. The time of your life is now.

Written Life Plan

If you were given a car in downtown Saint Petersburg, Russia, and told to drive to Tbilisi, Georgia, it is unlikely that you would reach your destination without a world map and some planning. The same is true of your life. If the goal of your life is personal happiness and the entire complex of achievements that happiness entails (family, friends, and career), you are not likely to get there without examining the body of human knowledge related to the subjects and doing some planning.

Most of us live our lives on automatic pilot. Many of us do not have a flight plan. As a member of the Fellowship of Reason you will get off automatic pilot and get back in control of your own life.

As a member of the Fellowship of Reason you will be encouraged to take a life "time" inventory and to write out a short statement of the major purposes of your life. Every day during private spiritual exercises you will be invited to reflect privately upon your life's purposes, and to evaluate whether you are spending your time in accordance with your life purposes.

As a result of the increased attention paid to your life purposes, you will make greater progress toward them.

FRIENDS

Members of the Fellowship of Reason, being rational individualists, will necessarily have values in common. As members we will have a mutual commitment to being gregarious hosts and hostesses to visitors and fellow members. We will be aggressively benevolent.

To newcomers to our area we will be a sanctuary of reason. To fellow members, our friends, who are suffering or celebrating life changes such as pregnancy, birth, graduation, marriage, career success, sickness, and death, we will offer support and encouragement. This is not altruism. This is voluntary exchange among friends to mutual benefit. We are creating a voluntary community of like-minded individuals in which one of the benefits we provide to each other is mutual aid and encouragement in good times and bad.

ENTERTAINMENT

As an alternative to indiscriminately watching broadcast television, the Fellowship of Reason will provide an opportunity to enjoy art and music representative of your values.

LONG RANGE VALUES

Because of the special training we offer to members, we expect that among our members the rates of teenage pregnancy, delinquency, crime, divorce, and stress-related sickness and death will be significantly lower than the population as a whole. We expect all our members to achieve financial independence despite high taxes and without regard to promised government entitlements. We expect all our members to attend to their personal health and fitness.

FELLOWSHIP OF REASON

Spread Freedom and Happiness

Over the years as others see our success, our philosophy of reason will spread. Our conviction that the highest of all values is individual human life will become universal. On that day, human freedom and happiness will be achieved for the entire world.

Home

Imagine what your home life was like as a child. Here is a brief account of an afternoon in a fictional home to refresh your memories.

Christine and Ephraim are the proud parents of four children, Francis, Lawrence, Ophelia, and Rachel.

On this beautiful spring day in April, Ephraim is preparing a wonderful dinner to celebrate his wife's birthday.

Christine has not yet returned from work and Ephraim is a little worried. Today, Christine was to have undergone her annual employee review. She has been concerned about it for weeks because her employer had announced that reductions in force would be necessary.

Francis, their youngest child (age four), is entertaining herself with her dolls in the living room. Lawrence (age nine) is learning about dinosaurs on the Internet for a class project. Ophelia (age thirteen) is in timeout because she had a tantrum when she got home from school. Ephraim hopes that Ophelia will be able to regain control of herself and rejoin the family after a few minutes of reflection. Rachel (age eighteen) is studying for her senior honors class in comparative religion. She is particularly interested in clarifying her own views on important ethical questions. Rachel has never felt pressured by her parents to choose a particular religion or philosophy though she knows her parents to be non-theists.

Not really very late, the mother, Christine, returns home with a big smile on her face. She calls the family all around and announces the results of her employee review—a raise and a promotion! The CEFLOR family is ecstatic.

As this fictional afternoon in the life of the CEFLOR family suggests, families engage in Celebrations, Entertainment, Fellowship, Learning, Ori-

177

entation with values, and Reflection. These values were identified in chapter 1 as some of the objective values provided by religious institutions. The Fellowship of Reason pursues these values as well.

The nature of home

It takes about twenty years to make a man or a woman. During that twenty years, one's parents are primary contributors to the "finished" product. Educational institutions contribute, as do other family members, friends, and acquaintances. Parents teach children and model good behavior. Older siblings teach younger siblings. Teachers teach students. By the time a young adult reaches age twenty he is more than ready to fly the nest. He is ready to try to make a life for himself.

The young adult is likely to notice some differences between his former life at home and his new life in the outside world. At home, from the time he was born until the time he departed as an adult, he was regarded by everyone as a work-in-progress, a being in the making. He was not expected to know everything. It was accepted that he was learning, slowly but surely, day by day. Everyone, from his parents, to his older brothers and sisters, to his teachers, was there to teach him, to correct him when he erred, to pick him up when he fell down. Now at work in the real world, he is expected to perform according to standards. If he fails, he will be fired.

At home, he was regarded as a superlative value by all of those with whom he came in contact. He remembers that even the most trivial of occurrences were celebrated in his family. When his own younger sister brought home her first finger-painting swirl from preschool, his parents proudly displayed it upon the refrigerator. No birthday went unnoticed. Now, his fellow employees do not know or care about his birthday. Only his family and his girlfriend remember, as they always have.

Entertainment, formerly a family affair, is a matter of his own invention these days—television by default.

He finds that the only friends he has are from his childhood days. The matter of making new friends he discovers is non-trivial work.

He finds, too, that his assumption that he was a "finished" product is false. Life changes. He changes. He finds there is much to learn and nobody to teach him. He must learn by himself or lose his way.

A cultural institution

Not surprisingly, our young man will be drawn to existing cultural institutions to supply the needs he discovers go unfulfilled or inadequately fulfilled now that he is outside his family home.

But which existing cultural institution will satisfy his needs? To the government he is a taxpaying statistic. To the university he is a race or a sex that will balance their affirmative action program. To an employer he is an input to production. To retail sellers of consumer goods he is a paying customer. To entertainment providers he is a ticket-holding member of the audience.

What our young man needs, what we all need, is to be valued as a complete person. Recognizing that there are different stages of life is an important part of being human. That one must constantly grow in knowledge and character, that is, spiritually and morally, is a fact. This requirement of spiritual and moral growth all through adult life means that one is forever a work-in-progress. Being appreciated as a unique whole includes the understanding that one is a work-in-progress.

Our young man also needs teachers and heroes to guide and inspire him in his spiritual and moral growth. Our young man needs a plan for his life and he needs to appreciate his present, his now.

As a child, the family provided for these needs at home. As an adult, friends cannot supply all of these human needs. Governments, universities, employers, stores, theaters cannot supply these needs. The cultural institution that has traditionally supplied these needs is the church. Unfortunately, as we have learned in this book, and as everyone who has read this far already knew, the church, and religions generally, have some serious defects.

Now there is the Fellowship of Reason.

Moral communities like the Fellowship of Reason are different from other social institutions. Governments exist by force. Universities, employers, retailers, and entertainment providers take inputs of labor and capital and create products for paying customers. Moral communities exist as an act of will by the members of the community. In order for moral communities to exist, the members must decide to join together to provide these services to one another. In moral communities, every member is both a producer and a customer. As a producer, a member might give a lecture or play an instrument or teach Sunday school or keep the nursery or make the Wednesday night supper or clean the restrooms or give money to help pay the rent or be someone's moral hero. As a customer, a member might enjoy the service or learn a moral lesson in Sunday school or play basketball in the gymnasium or be inspired by the moral courage of another or enjoy recognition by others of his successes in life or be reminded of the good things in his own life.

Because you are both the producer and the customer of the Fellowship of Reason, do not look for a Fellowship of Reason in your neighborhood. It must come from you, from your will, from your action. Will it. Decide it will be. Create it.

Theists are most welcome in the Fellowship of Reason. Everyone is, after all, is entitled to happiness! In the appendix, I discuss the obvious and fundamental difference between theists and non-theists.

Appendix — Non-theism

Matters of religion should never be matters of controversy. We neither argue with a lover about his taste, nor condemn him, if we are just, for knowing so human a passion. That he harbours it is no indication of a want of sanity on his part in other matters. But while we acquiesce in his satisfaction and are glad he has it, we need no argument to dissuade us from sharing it. —Santayana 1988, p. 226

The stroke of genius that allowed this ecclesiastical power to succeed was achieved when the pervasive human guilt over inadequacy and failure was connected to the universal human reality of desire, especially sexual desire. That connection was largely a Christian achievement. Now whenever sexual desire emerged, guilt became overwhelming. —Spong 1998, p. 90

Myth basically serves four functions. The first is the mystical function. . . realizing what a wonder the universe is, and what a wonder you are, and experiencing awe before this mystery. —Campbell 1988, p. 39

For it is simply an incontrovertible fact that, with the rise of modern science, the entire cosmological structure of the Bible and the Church has been destroyed and not the cosmological only but the historical as well. —Campbell 1990, p. 225

The reader will have certainly divined by now that the Fellowship of Reason does not worship any gods. Our philosophy of reason does not address the existence of gods for exactly the same reason that it does not address the existence of ghosts, goblins, witches, sorcerers, fairies, trolls, or devils. There is no evidence to suggest that any of these exist except as inventions of the human imagination. Non-theism is, therefore, but a footnote to our philosophy of reason.

Why then, you rightly ask, should an appendix address the subject of non-theism? The answer is simple. We want theists to join the Fellowship of Reason. For theists to want to join us, we will have to persuade them to our non-theistic view. Thus we set the goal of this appendix—to begin the process of showing our theistic friends that they may not *reason* to God.

NEGATIVE REASONS FOR THEISM

Faith of our fathers

Have you ever considered why so few children of religious people choose a religion different from their parents'? Children of Catholics become Catholics. Children of Jews become Jews. Children of Muslims become Muslims. Children of Protestants become Protestants. Children of Buddhists become Buddhists. Children of Hindus become Hindus. The basis of this fidelity to the "faith of our fathers" is *not* mindful choice. The basis of this fidelity is unwillingness to question authority—the authority of our parents, our peers, our teachers, religious dictates, the media, and society.

As infants and young children we should and must obey our parents because we have no capacity to make judgments for ourselves. During adolescence we become aware that we are beings separate from our parents. We begin to make some judgments for ourselves. As young adults, we must take full responsibility for our own lives. Many young adults are unaware that the lessons of childhood must be checked for validity. Learned religious beliefs are among the childhood lessons that should be validated by every adult. Religious beliefs should not be accepted on faith.

It is the thing to do

For many Americans, belief in God is simply the path of least resistance. It is the socially acceptable thing to do. It is safe, inexpensive, and undemanding. Many of these people do not go to church. They have no interest in debating the existence of God. God means to them the whole of existence or the ground of all being or the prime mover or the principle of benevolence in the world. In this form, a belief in God is harmless enough.

Infantilism

In chapter 10 I discussed the transition from infancy to childhood. The infant experiences herself as an adored queen served by gods. Some people are unwilling to grow beyond this stage of infantile dependency to adult self-responsibility. The analogy between the life of an infant and the fanaticized life of the religious person is quite strong. Just as an infant finds himself in the center of his parents' universe, so the religious person imagines that his life is of personal concern to God. Just as an infant learns that his parents respond to his every thought and desire, so the religious person believes in the efficacy of prayer. Just as an infant is not concerned about tomorrow, so a religious person is told not to worry about tomorrow. God will take care of him. ("See how the lilies of the field grow. They do not labor or spin." Matthew 6:28.) Just as a child receives loving, ever-patient discipline from his parents, so the religious person believes that even after committing the most horrible crimes his God will forgive him. Just as an infant believes that he has a loving, responsive, omnipotent, omniscient, and omnipresent parent, so the religious person believes he has a loving, responsive, omnipotent, omniscient, and omnipresent God. The religious person even calls his God a Heavenly Father. In the Catholic Church there is a Holy Mother.

Fear of death

"There are no atheists in foxholes," goes the saying. I have not been to war and do not presume to judge the mental lifeboats of terrified men in the face of incomprehensible horrors. I suppose that given the proper stimulus, the human mind can be tortured into many horrible shapes. George Orwell's futuristic novel *1984* illustrates how an efficient totalitarian government might make its victims puppets to the government's will. The Catholic Church's Inquisition (1231–1820 CE) exemplifies an historical attempt to mold human ideas by torture.

Fear of death causes many people to jump into the mental lifeboat called "theism." But death is nothing. Death is non-existence. There is

183

literally "nothing" to fear. I think there is something else at work in the fear of death.

If we examine the fear of death we will find hidden behind that fear a foreshadowing of guilt for not having lived our lives well. This is a fear greater than the fear of death. The failure to live our lives well is caused by failing to take responsibility for our own happiness by making our choices deliberately and by acting upon them, in short, by failing to live consciously. The central focus of the Fellowship of Reason is on living our lives well. The Fellowship of Reason advises us to follow our bliss, to make our lives' purposes explicit, to act to achieve those purposes, and, as a result, to achieve happiness.

Religion advises us to sacrifice our lives and property, to turn the other cheek to those who offend, to submit to authority, and to await our eternal reward in a non-existent heaven. The Fellowship of Reason offers the possibility of happiness on earth. Religion denies the possibility of happiness in this life in exchange for a happy, but non-existent afterlife.

The religious placebo for the fear of death is the belief in an afterlife. Unfortunately, the belief in an afterlife is positively harmful because it encourages lethargy with respect to this life. The Fellowship of Reason advises us not to waste the glorious fact of our existence upon a baseless hope for a second chance after death.

In summary, fear of death is an important reason for belief in God. For the religious, death is not so troublesome if it is merely a door to a better existence. It is comforting to imagine that one will be ultimately reunited with departed loved ones. A rational individualist knows that wishing does not make it so. The Fellowship of Reason's answer to fear of death is to live your life with passion now. Let nothing interfere with that sacred task.

Positive Reasons for Theism

Unquestioning obedience to authority, laziness, childishness, and fear of death are not the only motives for religious belief. There are positive values and experiences that actually exist to which the name of God is given: individualism, wonder, aesthetic ecstasy, and love. A philosophy of reason identifies and integrates these facts. But, we do not endorse the additional label, "God."

Christianity and individualism

Christianity has contributed to the elevation of the individual from prehistoric barbarism. Individualism is an objective virtue to which people are properly drawn. Historically, Christianity's individualistic component has been a strong draw for theists.

If Christianity is viewed in an historical context, it can be seen as an improvement from older times. Take, for example, the issue of sacrifice. Some primitive cultures engaged in human sacrifice and ritual cannibalism. The Old Testament forbade human sacrifice, but embraced the practice of animal sacrifice. This was progress. In the New Testament, Jesus is the final living sacrifice and saves mankind. More progress. (Theists still regularly celebrate the final human sacrifice in the cannibalistic ritual of Holy Communion in which the body and blood of Christ are symbolically consumed by the faithful.)

Another area of progress can be seen in the individualistic nature of the religion of the New Testament. Jesus is the savior of *individuals*. God becomes a *personal* God. He is no longer only the God of a chosen people, Israel, but now a *personal* savior who offers eternal life to *individuals*.

Here is a brutal example of Christian individualism. Skip to the next section if you are squeamish.

In order to compel the early Christian martyrs to renounce their belief in God and in Jesus, their persecutors publicly tortured them. The torture, the victims were told, would end if they publicly renounced their beliefs.

Consider the horrible story of the slave woman Blandina of Lyons [France] in the summer of 177 CE.

> All of us were in terror; and Blandina's earthly mistress, who was herself among the martyrs in the conflict, was in agony lest because of her bodily weakness she would not be able to make a bold confessor of her faith. Yet Blandina was filled with such power that even those who were taking turns to torture her in every way from dawn to dusk were weary and

exhausted. They themselves admitted that they were beaten, that there was nothing further they could do to her, and they were surprised that she was still breathing, for her entire body was broken and torn.

Later Blandina and her companions were taken into the amphitheater as victims of the gladiatorial games:

Blandina was hung on a post and exposed as bait for the wild animals that were let loose on her. She seemed to hang there in the form of a cross, and by her fervent prayer she aroused intense enthusiasm in those who were undergoing their ordeal... But none of the animals had touched her, and so she was taken down from the post and brought back to the jail to be preserved for another ordeal... tiny, weak, and insignificant as she was, she would give inspiration to her brothers... Finally, on the last day of the gladiatorial games, they brought back Blandina again, this time with a boy of fifteen named Ponticus. Every day they had been brought in to watch the torture of the others, while attempts were made to force them to swear by the pagan idols. And because they persevered and condemned their persecutors, the crowd grew angry with them, so that...they subjected them to every atrocity and led them through every torture in turn.

The boy died, but Blandina survived every torture. Finally, Blandina

was at last tossed into a net and exposed to a bull. After being tossed a good deal by the animal, she no longer perceived what was happening... Thus she too was offered in sacrifice, while the pagans themselves admitted that no woman had ever suffered so much in their experience (Musurillo 1972, pp. 67-81).

FELLOWSHIP OF REASON

Blandina's courage must certainly have been as amazing to the pagans as it is to the modern reader. The question, "What *power* could sustain Blandina through such suffering?," certainly occurred to the torturers and the audience at the gladiatorial games. The mystery of Blandina's courage and strength certainly sparked interest in Blandina's religion and earned for Christianity many converts.

Blandina was not the only Christian martyr. Like many people who have had the courage of their convictions even unto death, I suggest that the mystery of Blandina's courage and strength is explained by her own moral character, her personal independence, pride, and integrity.

To understand the workings of independence, pride, and integrity in Blandina's psychology, let us compare the gods of the Romans with Blandina's God. The Roman emperor of the time was regarded as one deity among others. Blandina was a slave and thus of very low status. She could hardly have had very positive feelings toward her emperor-god and the society in which she was a slave. On the other hand, the *personal* God of Christianity offered Blandina *personal* salvation. Jesus Christ came to earth and died for *her* sins. All Blandina needed do to achieve *personal* salvation was to believe in her God. Finally, Blandina found in Christianity institutional validation for her own personal experience of herself as valuable. Blandina *was* somebody who should be saved. Blandina *was* worthy. Her God cared about *her. She* could achieve the kingdom of heaven along with everyone else, slave and master alike. "There is neither Jew nor Greek, slave nor free, male nor female, for you are all one in Christ Jesus (Galatians 3:28)."

Christianity's granting of *status* to Blandina certainly must have been a powerful motive for her commitment to that faith. Christianity, the religion of brotherly love, kindness, forgiveness, and mercy, greatly elevates the spiritual status of human beings from their existential status as subjects of an emperor-god. Christianity holds that all human beings are *entitled* to love, kindness, forgiveness, and mercy. There is nothing so important in existence as individual human beings. (God is *outside* existence, having created it.)

Thus, Blandina became a Christian. When the pagans came to destroy her and to make her renounce *her* faith, she resisted to the death.

187

Blandina had decided that Christianity was for her. It spoke to her in a way that made sense. Christianity validated her own sense of self-worth. The pagans who tormented her unjustly were, in her mind and in ours, utterly despicable and evil.

Consider the moral alternative made apparent in the crucible of the Roman amphitheater. You could be a Roman citizen who, for entertainment (!) enjoyed watching other human beings tortured to death. Or, you could be an adherent of a religion that recognized the worth of individual human beings. The choice is not so difficult.

So, Blandina went to her hideous death in defiance of the Romans (independence) and in the knowledge that she was loyal to *her* convictions (integrity) and that she was morally superior (pride) to those who tortured her.

Seen in this light, Blandina was a person who honored herself and others and who had such independence, pride, and integrity that she was willing to die for her values. Blandina achieved the full measure of human greatness. Bless her.

However, the power that sustained Blandina was not the power of her almighty God. The power that sustained Blandina was the power of her own almighty self.

Mystery and wonder of the universe

Many theists regard their experience of the mystery and wonder of the universe as evidence of God. In fact, for many, their sense of awe and reverence in contemplation of the cosmos is *the* quintessential religious experience.

Let us consider four variations of this experience of mystery.

The first variation, and perhaps most banal, is the simple awe and humility some experience when looking at a clear night sky. They say: "Doesn't all of this make you feel small and insignificant?" Others are more eloquent: "From the psychological point of view, the contemplative experiences his abysmal inferiority to that which he approaches [the tremendous mystery of the universe], and his voice dies in speechlessness (Everson 1988, p. 27)."

The second variation is the realization that the universe is teeming with incredible phenomena, energy, and life. This idea is illustrated in this passage:

> For Nature itself holds the clue to the divine. In its myriad forms, the great plenitude of being is poured out, streaming from the womb of potentiality, exploding into act. A kind of metaphysical combustion seems smoldering in the fabric of things, a surge of incipient energy, breaking out of the bounds of its nuclear forms, and disappearing into the beyond. It is this transformation the poet celebrates (Everson 1988, p. 13).

A third variation, not as widely experienced, is the sense that the universe is itself a living being. This view is expressed in the following quotation:

> Another theme that has engaged my verses is the expression of a religious feeling that perhaps must be called pantheism, though I hate to type it with a name. It is the feeling—I will say the certainty—that the universe is one being, a single organism, one great life that includes all life and all things; and is so beautiful that it must be loved and reverenced; and in moments of mystical vision we identify ourselves with it (Jeffers 1956).

A fourth variation, referred to at the end of the last quotation, widely experienced and an epiphany actively sought through meditation is the sensation that you are one with the universe, as follows:

> I perceived everything to be somehow part of me. As I sat on the peak of the mountain looking out at the landscape falling away from me in all directions, it felt exactly as if what I had always known as my physical body was only the head of a much larger body consisting of everything else I could see. I experienced the entire universe looking out on itself through my eyes.

This perception induced a flash of memory. My mind raced backward in time, past the beginning of my trip to Peru, past my childhood and my birth. The realization was present that my life did not, in fact, begin with my conception and birth on this planet. It began much earlier with the formation of the rest of me, my real body, the universe itself (Redfield 1884, p. 98).

The realization that you share a kind of identity with the universe as a whole is a profound experience. In rational terms, a full comprehension of the concept "existence" necessitates the realization that you are one among all of the things that exist. Furthermore, you grasp that your matter, the actual, changing contents of your cells are literally taken from the raw materials of the universe. You are, literally, star dust. Finally, you sense that you have very much in common with every other human being of the 6 billion human beings presently on this planet. And, you are very much like the billions upon billions of human ancestors who preceded you.

This identification of yourself with all others and with the whole of existence is the mightiest of religious experiences. The experience can engender a profound sense of peace and brotherhood. "[T]he mystery of the *being* of that thing [a tree, a bird, anything] is identical with the mystery of the being of the universe—and of yourself (Campbell 1990, p. 196)."

The emotions of awe and wonder when contemplating the universe are aesthetic responses to beauty. Aesthetics is the study of beauty and psychological responses to it. Religions recreate these aesthetic experiences using literature, art (magnificent buildings, stained glass, golden altars, beautiful garments, and incense), and music.

Poetry can elicit a similar aesthetic response. For example:

> I am past childhood, I look at this ocean and the fishing birds,
> the streaming skerris, the shining water,
>
> The foam-heads, the exultant dawn-light going west, the pelicans, their huge wings half folded, plunging like stones.

FELLOWSHIP OF REASON

> Whatever it is catches my heart in its hands, whatever it is
> make me shudder with love
>
> And painful joy and the tears prickle... The Greeks were not
> its inventors (Jeffers 1938, p. 602).

Our philosophy of reason aspires to replace religion in the hearts of mankind. One of our greatest challenges is to embrace, explain, and replicate these profound aesthetic responses to existence in Celebration.

Personal experience of god

There are people who claim to have had a visitation by an angel or the Holy Spirit. Sometimes this information is communicated to the listener in confidence, friend to friend. In this situation the confidence should be treated with profound respect. I have had friends and acquaintances relate experiences of this type. One dear friend at a very low moment in his life was walking alone at night on Christmas Eve. His ex-wife lived in another state with their children. He was considering suicide. He encountered a white light in the shape of a lady, who my friend described as his guardian angel. The angel offered him solace and gave him strength to survive that night. Another acquaintance related that one night in the desert under the influence of marijuana she had a vision of heaven. Both of these stories were related to me in confidence and with the deepest sincerity. I do not doubt that my dear friend and my acquaintance believed their stories.

There are three reasons why I do not accept these reports as evidence of the existence of God:

The incidents reported contradict all the data of my experience. I have never seen an angel. I have never personally visited heaven. I know of no authentic report of such an event. The reports contradict all I know about the laws of physics.

My dear friend was not an unbiased witness. He was under severe psychological distress because of the absence of friends and family on the most important family day of the year. My acquaintance was under the influence of drugs.

The reported events cannot be repeated or demonstrated to others. They are non-objective.

It is my considered judgment that my dear friend and my acquaintance misinterpreted natural psychological events in their minds and reported those events as supernatural.

There are people who claim to have regular interactive conversations with God. Historically, such people have been called prophets. Most people who make this claim to me do not claim to be prophets. Their conversations with God have only personal relevance. I respectfully decline to accept this as evidence of the existence of God.

We all have "conversations" with ourselves when we think. "Should I do this? What will happen if I do that? Why do I feel such and such a way?" If our thought processes are successful, our minds, not God, will supply us with answers. It is my judgment that this is all that is happening with people who claim to have regular personal conversations with God. A profound respect for the natural capacities of the human mind is certainly appropriate. The human mind is not supernatural.

Fear of irremediable injustice

Injustice is to be resisted. But, sometimes the bad guys get away. Religious people find comfort in the fantasy that a Cosmic Cop will punish the bad guys.

The best response to this type of thinking I have read is this:

> The idea of a personal God, like one of us writ large, is fraught with difficulty. If this God is omnipotent, he could have prevented the Holocaust. If he was unable to stop it, he is impotent and useless; if he could have stopped it and chose not to, he is a monster. Jews are not the only people who believe that the Holocaust put an end to conventional theology (Armstrong 1994, p. 376).

We will have to muddle on fighting injustice ourselves without the help of the Cosmic Cop. (Perhaps millions of words have been written about the problem of evil, which religious scholars call theodicy.)

Love or grace

Good things happen. The love a parent experiences for her child is a good thing. Romantic love is a good thing. Sexual ecstasy is a good thing. Intimate friendships are good.

Many people claim that these powerful experiences are evidence of God. I do not get the connection. It is interesting that while no theist is willing to blame his God for any undeserved evil inflicted upon him or others, all theists credit their God for all good.

Unitive experience

One time as a teenager I was sunning myself on the beach in front of my grandmother's house. I had no worries. I felt great. Suddenly, I had an acute awareness of the sun on my back, the sand near my face, the intense blue sky, the sound of the waves lapping the shore, and a sense of profound well-being. I still remember that experience vividly now thirty-five years later. A few years ago, I was sitting in a garden with my wife. We were visiting Provence in June. I had a similar acute awareness. Both of these experiences were extremely pleasant and vivid. I hope to have many more like them.

Other people who have had this type of experience have described it as seeming to be at one with the universe. It has been named the "unitive experience" by Gerald G. May, MD, in his book *Will and Spirit: A Contemplative Psychology* (1987). Abraham Harold Maslow called them "peak experiences" in his book *Religions, Values, and Peak Experiences* (1976). Plotinus (205?–270), author of *Enneads*, spent his life in search of this experience. One of my teachers says that Plotinus claimed to have had three such experiences in his lifetime. This is the quintessential religious experience. It is the goal of meditation. It is a true and wonderful experience.

I respectfully disagree that this experience is evidence of God. It *is* evidence that ecstasy is a part of the human experience.

Church for the children

Many people go to church for the sake of their children's moral education. As a matter of fact, until the creation of the Fellowship of Reason, the church *was* the only place to receive formal moral education. Today the Fellowship of Reason offers formal moral education to adults and children alike. We intend to compete directly with the religions of the world for this market.

The Greatest Obstacle to Non-theism: God-Esteem

In the last thirty years, the importance of self-esteem to successful human functioning has come to scientific light. Psychology now teaches that in order to function, a person must have self-esteem or a substitute. The Catholic Church learned long ago that an effective way to control its members was to undermine self-esteem and provide a substitute. Catholics are taught from a very young age that they are hopeless sinners. They are indoctrinated with the idea of Original Sin. The Original Sin was Adam's taking of fruit from the tree of knowledge. For that sin Adam and Eve were driven from the Garden of Eden. What every newborn human child has to do with that sin and why she should be held accountable for it is inexplicable. It is a horrible inversion of morality to blame anyone for an act she did not commit, that she had no control over, and that happened in a mythical time and place. But this is precisely the poison that every young Catholic child is fed.

A young Catholic has been taught from the earliest moments of life by her Catholic parents and by the Church that extramarital sex and sex with no procreative intention are evil. As yet unexperienced sexual desire and supposed innate human wickedness are artificially cemented together by the teaching of the Church. When she enters puberty her body provides her proof positive that she is evil, just as she has been told. Her body is interested in sex! *Quelle horreur*!

The young Catholic, who has been taught an unearned guilt from birth, now has proof from her own body that she is in fact evil. The young Catholic suffers enormous guilt. Normally a person is disabled by guilt. But the Church offers a way out. By confession, prayer, and service to God the young Catholic can receive the healing love of God. Gotcha! The Church undermines self-esteem and substitutes God-esteem. God-esteem is given upon conditions that the Church sets. The trap is closed. The servant is secured.

A victim of a lifetime of guilt-conditioning by the Church has a substantially diminished self-esteem and will not, as a matter of personal psychological survival, give up his substitute, God-esteem.

In this section I speak only of a small group of people who have been seriously injured by religion's greatest evil—the connection of human sexual desire with guilt.

Dissembling Non-theists

Another group of so-called believers is the non-theists who claim to believe in God so that they can fit into a theistic culture. While hard to detect, this group is, I suspect, quite large. There are two related reasons to misrepresent one's non-theism. The first is that the word atheist is almost synonymous in our language with evil. This equation is due in part to the historical fact that Marxism, a patently evil philosophy, is atheistic, and in part to the fact that there has been, until now, no coherent non-theistic moral theory. The dominant secular theories have heretofore been nihilism or subjectivism. The related reason to misrepresent your non-theism is that atheists are discriminated against in our society. In order to belong to and participate in certain organizations, like the Boy Scouts, or the Girl Scouts, one must believe in God. Before the existence of the Fellowship of Reason, it was impossible to enjoy the values of fellowship, celebration, fellowship, personal reflection, reorientation with moral values, enjoyment of art, and ethics in an institutional setting.

Non-theists v. Atheists

We are not atheists. By atheist I mean a person who advocates the non-existence of God. We, the members of the Fellowship of Reason, do not define ourselves by that which we do not believe, but by what we do believe. We believe in this earth, this life, the pursuit of happiness, and in all of the good people who inhabit this earth.

Faith v. Reason

There is no "reason" to believe in God. Belief in God is a matter of faith. Faith is the antithesis of reason. We are not a fellowship of faith. Since there is no evidence of the existence of God, our philosophy of reason is non-theistic. The Fellowship of Reason worships no gods.

> **Let me conclude this appendix and the book by stating unequivocally that theists are welcome in the Fellowship of Reason. We wish everyone happiness on earth.**

References

Aristotle. *Nicomachean Ethics.* Translated by H. Rackham. Cambridge, Mass.: Harvard University Press.

Armstrong, Karen. 1994. *A History of God: The 4000-Year Quest of Judaism, Christianity and Islam.* New York: Ballantine Books.

Bloom, Allan. 1987. *The Closing of the American Mind: How Higher Education Has Failed Democracy and Impoverished The Soul's of Today's Students.* New York: Simon and Schuster.

Branden, Nathaniel. July 1962. "Benevolence versus Altruism." In *The Objectivist Newsletter.* Vol. 1, No. 7.

———. 1971. *The Psychology of Self-Esteem.* New York: Bantam Books.

———. 1999. *The Art of Living Consciously: The Power of Awareness to Transform Everyday Life.* New York: Simon and Schuster.

Campbell, Joseph. 1972. *The Hero with a Thousand Faces.* Princeton: Princeton University Press.

———. 1976. *The Masks of God: Primitive Mythology.* New York: Penguin Books.

———. 1990. *The Flight of the Wild Gander: Explorations in the Mythological Dimension.* New York: HarperCollins.

———. 1991. *The Power of Myth with Bill Moyers.* New York: Anchor Books.

Courtois, Stéphane, Nicolas Werth, Jean-Louis Panné, Andrzej Paczkowski, Karel Bartošek, and Jean-Louis Margolin eds. 1999. *The Black Book of Communism: Crimes, Terror, Repression.* Translated by Jonathan Murphy and Mark Kramer. Cambridge, Mass.: Harvard University Press.

Csikszentmihalyi, Mihaly. 1991. *Flow: the Psychology of Optimal Experience.* New York: HarperCollins.

———. 1997. *Finding Flow: The Psychology of Engagement with Everyday Life.* New York: Basic Books.

Everson, William. 1988. *The Excesses of God: Robinson Jeffers as a Religious Figure*. Stanford, Cal.: Stanford University Press.

Frazier, Charles. 1998. *Cold Mountain: A Novel*. New York: Vintage Books.

Graber, David M. October 22, 1989. Review of *Mother Nature as Hothouse Flower: The End of Nature*, by Bill McKibben. In *Los Angles Times Book Review*.

Hadot, Pierre. 1995. *Philosophy as a Way of Life*. Translated by Michael Chase. Malden, Mass.: Blackwell Publishers.

———. 1998. *The Inner Citadel: The Meditations of Marcus Aurelius*. Translated by Michael Chase. Cambridge, Mass.: Harvard University Press.

Jeffers, Robinson. 1938. "Hellenistic. In *The Selected Poetry of Robinson Jeffers*. New York: Random House.

———. 1956. "The Poet in Democracy." In *Themes in My Poems*. San Francisco: The Book Club of California. Cited from Everson 1988, p. 15.

Kelley, David. 1996. *Unrugged Individualism: The Selfish Basis of Benevolence*. Poughkeepsie, New York: Institute for Objectivist Studies.

Marx, Karl. 1848. *Manifesto of the Communist Party*.

Maslow, Abraham Harold. 1976. *Religions, Values, and Peak Experiences*. New York: Penguin Books.

May, Gerald G. 1987 *Will and Spirit: A Contemplative Psychology*. New York: HarperCollins.

Monroe, Kristen Renwick. 1996. *The Heart of Altruism: Perceptions of a Common Humanity*. Princeton: Princeton University Press.

Musurillo, Herbert Anthony, ed. 1972. "Martyrs of Lyon" 9. In *The Acts of the Christian Martyrs*. Oxford: Oxford University Press.

Nelson, O. T. 1977. *The Girl Who Owned A City*. New York: Laurel-Leaf Books.

Norton, David L. 1976. *Personal Destinies: A Philosophy of Ethical Individualism*. Princeton: Princeton University Press.

Ortega y Gasset, José. 2000. *Meditations on Quixote*. Translated by Evelyn Rugg and Diego Marin. Chicago: University of Illinois Press.

Prager, Dennis. 1999. *Happiness is a Serious Problem: A Human Nature Repair Manual*. New York: Regan Book.
Rand, Ayn. 1943. *The Fountainhead*. New York: The Bobbs-Merrill Company.
———. 1957. *Atlas Shrugged*. New York: Random House.
———. 1961. *The Virtue of Selfishness*. New York: Signet.
———. 1975. *The Romantic Manifesto*. New York: Signet.
Redfield, James. 1994. *The Celestine Prophecy*. New York: Warner Books.
Reeve, Christopher. 1999. *Still Me*. New York: Ballantine Books.
Robinson, James M., ed. 1990. *The Nag Hammadi Library in English*. New York: HarperCollins.
Sagan, Carl. 1997. *Contact*. New York: Pocket Books.
Santayana, George. 1988. *The Life of Reason*. Amherst, New York: Prometheus Books.
Schrödinger, Erwin. 1961. *My View of the World*. Woodbridge, Conn.: Ox Bow Press.
Smith, Adam. 1970. *The Wealth of Nations*. New York: Penguin Books.
Spinoza, Baruch (Benedict). 1954. *The Philosophy of Spinoza*. New York: Random House.
Spong, John Shelby. 1998. *Why Christianity Must Change or Die: A Bishop Speaks to Believers in Exile*. New York: HarperCollins.
Vogler, Christopher. 1992. *The Writer's Journey: Mythic Structure for Storytellers & Screenwriters*. Studio City, Cal.: Michael Weise Productions.

To order additional copies of this book, contact:
Xlibris Corporation
1-888-7-XLIBRIS
www.Xlibris.com
Orders@Xlibris.com